# The Childhood of Jesus in Twelve Years

*How It Affects Your Child and Your Parental Responsibility*

## SOPHIA WILLIAM

authorHOUSE®

*AuthorHouse™*
*1663 Liberty Drive*
*Bloomington, IN 47403*
*www.authorhouse.com*
*Phone: 1-800-839-8640*

*First published by AuthorHouse    10/12/2011*

*ISBN: 978-1-4670-0178-6 (sc)*

*Printed in the United States of America*

*Any people depicted in stock imagery provided by Thinkstock are models, and such images are being used for illustrative purposes only.*
*Certain stock imagery © Thinkstock.*

*This book is printed on acid-free paper.*

*Because of the dynamic nature of the Internet, any web addresses or links contained in this book may have changed since publication and may no longer be valid. The views expressed in this work are solely those of the author and do not necessarily reflect the views of the publisher, and the publisher hereby disclaims any responsibility for them.*

*All scripture quotations are taken from the New King James Version of the Bible unless otherwise indicated.*

*The Childhood of Jesus in Twelve Years:*
*How It Affects Your Child and Your Parental Responsibility*

*Sophia William*

Praise, honour, and glory are to God the Father of our Lord Jesus Christ who has given me the ability to put this on paper. The Bible reminds us, *'For it is God who works in you both to will and to do for His good pleasure'* (Philippians 2:13).

I have written this book in dedication and in prayer to all children that, as they grow and develop, they may experience every moment of happiness and achievement in life. May all children explore the world around them with confidence, handle everything that their hands touch with trust, take every step and movement in life with freedom, and execute all their dealings with peace. May every child grow in wisdom as he or she embraces the world. May the suggestions in this book be Read, Rediscovered, Reconsidered, Recalled, and Reformed by those who are seeking to keep, follow after, pray for, speak for, and hearken to what Jesus and His parents have to offer the world today.

# ACKNOWLEDGEMENTS

I thank my husband, William, for his great support and encouragement. I express my gratitude to our two children, Jesse and Deborah, who have nicknamed this book 'the child.' I appreciate sister Tandie, who has kept asking me to write more articles after her reading and liking my very first story. Thanks to brother Francis for giving me ideas that improved my writing speed. Thanks to the management team and the members of the Kenya Community Association Liverpool for voicing belief in my writing talent at one of the meetings that was held in Liverpool. Thanks to sisters Rukia, Anzaye and Dorothy, who greatly rejoiced about the production of this book without a glimpse of its existence. Thanks to the Ushirika women who have stood with me in many ways. Congratulations to you who are reading this book.

# CONTENTS

# INTRODUCTION

Every parent who is reading this should be aware that every child is already wise in what the world calls 'the child's wisdom.' As your children grow and develop, do not let this wisdom that is in them dwindle away, stagnate, or die. Jesus was a Child just like your child. '*And Jesus increased in wisdom and stature, and in favour with God and men*' (Luke 2:52). Just as Jesus experienced childhood, so will your child. His childhood entailed three distinct and inseparable growth elements—namely, growth in wisdom, increase in stature, and attainment of favour in the sight of God and humanity. This wisdom that your child needs as he or she transcends from childhood into adulthood has already been provided and is available for him or her to attain it. '*If any of you lacks wisdom, let him ask of God, who gives to all liberally and without reproach, and it will be given to him*' (James 1:5). It is vital to grow in wisdom, and this wisdom is there for those who ask for it. God is our Father, and we can draw from Him the wisdom needed to bring up our children. As you read on, you will find a clear indication that it is important to possess and apply wisdom in our childrearing.

*Hear, my children, the instruction of a father, and give attention to know understanding; for I give you good doctrine: Do not forsake my law. When I was my father's son, tender and the only one in the sight of my mother, he also taught me, and said to me: 'Let your heart retain my words; keep my commands, and live. Get wisdom! Get understanding! Do not forget, nor turn away from the words of my mouth. Do not forsake her, and she will preserve you; love her, and she will keep you. Wisdom is the principal thing; therefore get wisdom. And in all your getting, get understanding. Exalt her, and she will promote you; she will bring you honor, when you embrace her. She will place on your head an ornament of grace; a crown of glory she will deliver to you.' Hear, my son, and receive my sayings, and the years of your life will be many. I have taught you in the way of wisdom; I have led you in right paths. When you walk, your steps will not be hindered, and when you run, you will not stumble. Take firm hold of instruction, do not let go; keep her, for she is your life. Do not enter the path of the wicked, and do not walk in the way of evil. Avoid it, do not travel on it; turn away from it and pass on. For they do not sleep unless they have done evil; and their sleep is taken away unless they make someone fall. For they eat the bread of wickedness, and drink the wine of violence. But the path of the just is like the shining sun, that shines ever brighter unto the perfect day. The way of the wicked is like darkness; they do not know what makes them stumble. My son, give attention to my words; incline your ear to my sayings. Do not let them depart from your eyes; keep them in the midst of your heart; for they are life to those who find them, and health to all their flesh. Keep your heart with all diligence, for out of it spring the issues of life. Put away from you a deceitful mouth, and put perverse lips far from you. Let your eyes look straight ahead, and your eyelids look right before you. Ponder the path of your feet, and let all your ways be established. Do not turn to the right or to the left; remove your foot from evil.* (Proverbs 4)

I myself was born into a non-Christian family. I converted to Christianity during my high school days. My conversion followed a viewing of the film, *The Crucifixion of Jesus*, in a Christian Union Fellowship at school. I softly whispered the following words that gave meaning to and started a change in my life: 'Lord Jesus, I believe you underwent this pain for my sake. Forgive my trespasses and control my life. I accept you as the Lord and Saviour of my life. I welcome you in my life. Amen.' From the day of my confession until now, God has enabled me to walk through the journey of Christian faith.

I still have the tendency to believe that those children who are brought up in Christian families are privileged to start knowing the Lord Jesus Christ earlier in their life. It is an honour for them to hear of their friend, Jesus, early in life, and parents had better keep hold on this. I learned about Christ at a distance and with precaution, lest I offended my own family. All in all, I have found the Lord Jesus Christ to be a faithful friend. Thus, I admire Mary and Joseph's way of bringing up their child. I am convinced that if children are brought up in this supposedly *old way* (according to the 'modernized world'), then they will not be denied the place of God in their lives. Mary and Joseph's style of bringing up their child has won my life, and I prefer it for child upbringing. I would not want any child to have similar feelings and wishes I have always had—the wish to have known Jesus earlier in my life. I am glad that when I found Jesus in my late teenage life, I found a true friend, a good teacher, and a real mentor. It would have been more wonderful to have known such a person earlier in my life. I would recommend that every parent imitate Mary and Joseph's way of parenting. I did not grow up going to Sunday school as some of you parents did, and you need take this to have happened for your good and for that of your children too. It was and it is a privilege to walk a pattern that our Lord Jesus walked.

I personally believe that the blessings that the Bible speaks of were hidden quite far from my grasp. It was not until I received Jesus Christ as my Lord and Saviour that I started partaking in these blessings. The value that I have attached to my conversion compels me to put on paper what you are now reading. Neither parent nor child should think of despising what he or she already has. I led a life of emptiness, fear, and uncertainty before I met Christ. My life and hope for the future changed for good from the moment I found Jesus. Taking our children to the house of God is one way of channelling them towards finding Jesus—the hero of their life. While walking on the earth, Jesus loved children and rebuked His disciples for the habit of forbidding parents from bringing children to Him. Jesus still loves children, and we do wrong when we deny children access to their friend, Jesus.

It is easy to believe in the fictional Superman, but Jesus is more than Superman. It is good that children can identify their parents or other significant people as the champions in their life, but in comparison to who Jesus is, the former are only humans with limitations. One time I learned a lesson about earthly heroes—they can easily slip away without warning. I learned this from my two heroes; my beloved mum and my dear grandmother who both passed away in a period of seven months apart. It was devastating.

They never managed to fight back and stay with me. I still needed them but they were gone. This is because they were only human beings with limitations. A situation similar to mine was about to befall the human race when Jesus died on the cross, but, He arose from the dead. Unlike for my mum and grandma, Jesus' death was sacrificial. He willed to die for humanity. He gave His life to buy ours, *'just as the Son of Man did not come to be served, but to serve, and to give His life a ransom for many.'* (Mathew 20: 28). Jesus has always been there for every one and He can be trusted. He commanded His disciples to go to all nations with the instruction of *'teaching them to observe all things that I have commanded you; and lo, I am with you always, even to the end of the age* (Mathew 28:20). By starting a relationship with Jesus, I started a new life, and my adoption into the family of God began. I have found this experience to be real. *'Therefore, if anyone is in Christ, he is a new creation; old things have passed away; behold, all things have become new'* (2 Corinthians 5:17).

The earthly parents of Jesus have attracted my whole being when it comes to how they brought up their child in a Godly way. Every family on earth offers an environment that has beliefs and values for its advantage, but just as iron sharpens iron, Mary and Joseph can sharpen most parents. It is for this cause that I wouldn't like any parent or child to miss out on the best suggestions on offer in this book.

My husband and I have young children who are still in their tender ages and stages of growth and development, and Mary and Joseph have become our parenting role models. We live in days of civilization and sophistication, but as parents, we are confident that recommending the Mary and Joseph's parenting style is an ideal idea. As you read on, you will discover that approaching life with the Lord Jesus

Christ at the core of everything guarantees victory. Jesus overcame all the odds of childhood life, and thus, only He can offer what our children need in life. We must, therefore, not forget to learn from the parents that brought Him up.

I invite every parent to meet the parents who set an ultimate example in parenting. I welcome all parents and children to meet the child who triumphed in life. The supposedly ancient parenting style of Mary and Joseph can save the human race a lot of heartaches. This parenting style, if applied today, increases the chances of our children knowing and being acquainted with their friend Jesus early in life.

Jesus loves children, and children love Jesus; this is reflected in the way children embrace Christmas—the birthday of their friend. Children have always been thrilled with and interested in the celebration of Christmas. Parents need to take this opportunity of festivity to introduce their children to the birthday boy at Christmas. I am sure that all the people who show up at any birthday party always do convey their best wishes for the child whose birthday party they are attending. The other thing that we do is to wish the child a long life. If the child is to live many years, then the provision of favourable conditions from the environment and from those people around the child becomes necessary. Jesus was born in a manger, but He needs a place to grow; and He grows in the hearts of people. I am sure we do not want Him to freeze in the manger when it is winter! Leaving any child unsheltered, and especially in the outside cold, is against the health and safety conditions of today. Inasmuch as we embrace the birth of Jesus through the celebration of Christmas, it is our responsibility to provide a suitable environment for His growth—this can only be in one's tender heart.

It should, however, be remembered that the child Jesus can only grow in our hearts and those of our children if we make a choice and give Him permission to do so. It is witnessed of Jesus, '*Behold, I stand at the door and knock. If anyone hears My voice and opens the door, I will come in to him and dine with him, and he with Me*' (Revelation 3:20). Inasmuch as the Christmas celebration should glow, the growth of the birthday child behind this celebration should not be hindered or ignored.

At any gathering, and especially during partying, the adults normally gang up on their own because of the common interests that they share; the same happens with children. This means that, if Jesus was here on the earth during a Christmas celebration, our children would be gathered around Him and cut cake with Him. He is the birthday boy, and children would have a lot of common interests to share with Him. Children identify best with other children, and that is why I call upon parents to set their children free in order for them to fully interact and socialize with the birthday child.

Mary and Joseph are the parents at any Christmas party, and they have the best advice that they can give to those who are ready to take it on board. Their child grew up like any other child, but He attracted the attention of the entire world. I am sure every parent would be eager to know how Mary and Joseph made it as parents. Only ignorance or self pride would cause a parent to attend a celebrity's party without wishing to know the keys to the named celebrity's success (and that of his or her parents). I am sure that every adult and child would be interested in knowing more about the celebrity and, even later, might decide to copy the celebrity's lifestyle. It is only natural and healthy for parents to interact with each other, learn from each other, and share experiences. It is, however, advisable for parents to take care when it comes to the advice they receive and from whom they receive it. If what you are now reading is what you would have loved to hear from Mary and Joseph, and if this would be of any help to you or anyone around you, then take it in; it is all about their child. Most parents want to hear from each other, but the words of those parents who have good things to offer about parenting—such as Mary and Joseph, interest the hearers most. This is why we should not ignore Mary and Joseph from today onwards. It is only wise for parents and those who are planning to be parents to realize that iron sharpens iron and these parents want to sharpen us.

If any particular party has to begin, and if those in attendance of the occasion have to share in and encounter the burst of true pleasure, praise, laughter, and joy, then every outlet will have to be opened so that the flow of freedom and permission for maximum participation are availed. Parents need to allow their children to cut the birthday cake, sing the birthday song, dance to the birthday rhythm, and play with the birthday child. On many occasions, the birthday child and the children at the party want to explore together; and withholding them or setting very hard rules for the day only leads to the children experiencing frustration. For anyone who is reading this book, the freedom of choice of ideas is permitted.

My purpose for picking the Christmas topic is to take parents through the journey of how it would have felt to accompany their children to every birthday party that Jesus celebrated—mainly those celebrations that occurred before He turned twelve. I believe that, given the opportunity to do so, most parents would be interested in wanting to know how Mary and Joseph succeeded in raising their child. The beauty of the childhood of Jesus has never and will never fade. During most gatherings, people end up forming secluded groups, classified according to age range and shared interests, and this happens without any prior arrangements. This makes me think that, at such a party, every child would have wanted to associate with Jesus, and every parent would have sought to associate with Mary and Joseph.

The core reason for writing this book is to try and draw out vital matching elements in the parenting of Mary and Joseph and our parenting. Jesus was a child just like your child. His parents, Mary and Joseph, were parents just like us. The angel of the Lord separately spoke to both of them about their unborn child. They both responded in ways that revealed the human weaknesses in them. Inasmuch as it is good to know your child, it's also good to know yourself. Both Mary and Joseph had personal limitations, but despite those limitations, they succeeded in their parenting. The angel of God appeared to Mary, the mother of Jesus, with the message of her conception. Her first response towards the angle and the conveyed message was as follows: '*But when she saw him, she was troubled at his saying, and considered what manner of greeting this was*' (Luke 1:29).

Mary was troubled and considered this message within. In most cases, when prospective parents receive the message that they have conceived a child, they are eager and joyous, but in the case of Mary, she was in a situation that caused her to be troubled. She was a virgin and betrothed to Joseph, but before they came together, she received this message about the child that she was to bear. There are times when some parents get troubled about the child they are expecting or about the child they are parenting, but whatever hurdle one is caught in, it is good to know that, '*For with God nothing will be impossible'* (Luke 1: 37). There are those anxious moments when some parents may not understand the titles with which their children have been labelled. Yet for some parents, they may have limited ability regarding the situations they find themselves in at the time of expecting their unborn child; but Mary has exemplified victory. Joseph was also in a similar thoughtful and reconsidering state. He had issues of concern about Mary and the baby she was bearing, but he overcame these issues. The Bible tells us: *'But while he thought about these things, behold, an angel of the Lord appeared to him in a dream . . .'* (Matthew 1:20). These two parents have paved a way in the parenting journey. The angel of the Lord appeared to them on separate occasions, but both of them, at their own choice, had to show dependence on and belief in God. God was at hand to help and see these parents through. It is never too early or too late for parents to start receiving God's instructions about their growing child. God's intention for the child is always for protection, just as we hear Him saying through the angel. *'Now when they had departed, behold, an angel of the Lord appeared to Joseph in a dream, saying, "Arise, take the young Child and His mother, flee to Egypt, and stay there until I bring you word; for Herod will seek the young Child to destroy Him."'* (Matthew 2:13). In the same way, God is at hand to help every parent today. This help will always be available, but parents are called upon to stretch and reach out for it. This is an indication that parents need to put careful consideration into what they hear about their child, from whom they hear it, and how they respond to what they hear. What can you learn from the parenting example of Mary and Joseph?

# PART I

## The Foundations

# 1

## Parenting before the Child's
## Twelfth Birthday

The foundation laid for the child from birth until the age of twelve is of fundamental importance. This shapes your child's future. Laying a good foundation for young children helps them to safely go through the theoretical milestones of growth and development, before stepping into a purposeful adulthood. The age of twelve is the stepping stone into the teenage years—the dividing wall between childhood and adulthood. The stone underneath may seem easy to get over, but the wall ahead may be hard to climb. The trend of change that gaps these two stages of life can be likened to climbing up to the topmost part of one ladder then suddenly being required to change onto a second ladder whilst maintaining the height. The linkup between these two gaps may be too narrow or too wide for your child to cope with, since there is no chance of coming down to recollect steps and actions before continuing. If proper balancing, confidence, and concentration are required in taking the step of transferring from one ladder to the next, then it becomes necessary for parents to ensure their children's safety. The actual transformation from childhood into adulthood lies within every individual child, but boosting the child's self-esteem enables him or her to confidently take the first required initiative. For example, when a child physically climbs and transfers between ladders, it is the parent's responsibility to firmly hold the two ladders whilst encouraging, reassuring, and standing by the child in order to ensure a simple and a danger-free transfer. The dangers between the gapping spaces should be avoided by the parent forming the bridge on which the child can walk. Underneath the two high ladders, there is hard earth that may injure your child should he or she fall, or a massive water surface in which your child may drown. Since no caring parent would wish or wait for a fatal accident to befall his or her child, in the case that your child should fall, your soft hands should always be available for him or her to grab. Parents should not leave a child on his or her own. This is mainly because parents stand in a better position of knowing their child's abilities and tolerances. Children need regular encouragement, reassurance, praise and rewards from parents. Only then will the child's self-esteem antenna be raised. The laying of a good foundation for a child can encompass the following provisions from parents:

1. FOOD—Focus, Order, Own, Discipline
2. WATER—Welcome, Acknowledge, Train, Enhance, Respect
3. AIR—Advise, Inspire, Recreate
4. SHELTER—Support, Harbour, Equip, Lead, Teach, Extol, Relate
5. HEAT—Hope, Expand, Achieve, Trust
6. LOVE—Lift, Oversee, Value, Ease

Throughout your child's journey of growth and development, you should retain guardianship in continuity, since children face greater exposure to the influences and the challenges of the big world as they advance in age. As the child approaches the age of twelve, parents should aim at building his or her independence and confidence. These two qualities aid in helping a child positively and purposefully step out into the world ahead. This, in turn, ensures safe transfer from the family enclosure and landing in the world exposure; these two distinct environments are totally different from each other. Imparting the above vital qualities in your child is one way of showing that you hold his or her hand and together you can climb over all obstacles and achieve common goals. At the age of twelve, most children decline the physical holding of their hands when walking and even the company of their parents. The child would rather miss out on things or stay behind than be accompanied to places. This is because, to a child, having to be escorted by an adult is embarrassing; the child feels that he or she is being denied the ability to feel and act grown up. It is most appreciated if parents keep some distance and allow their child some breathing space. However, the whole idea is to know when you are needed and when you are not needed, avoiding the extremes of being too nosy or too ignorant. Every child, and especially at the crucial and ultimate preteen phase, needs the assurance that there is somebody besides him or herself who he or she can trust, lean upon, and call upon. This is an ultimate age because the child is about to start experiencing hormonal changes that befall teenagers. The trust that both the child and the parent build in each other should be able to fix the parent as the first reference point. The parent is a first reference point when the child calls upon him or her and tells him or her things without being asked or prompted. A child has yet more knowledge and skills to acquire, and parents ought to be in the front line when it comes to equipping their children with know-how about handling life affairs.

The biological body processes and changes that set off in most twelve year olds can be overwhelming. However, if parents or guardians take every possible opportunity to prepare the child psychologically, then they will help to lessen and protect the child from most harsh experiences and peer group influences, essentially eradicating these influences by helping him or her to avoid them. If your child never gets information and hears instructions from you, then he or she will get and hear it from somewhere else; the context of which may not be of your liking.

This does not mean that you unnecessarily and insensitively force information onto your child. If you give too much information to the child, it becomes confusing. It is good to remember that children's minds are not fully developed to handle hard information. Since it is hard to know what a child can filter or store in his or her mind, we should give our children information in stages. This information should be weighed for significance, considering its applicability and using it only for its intended course. This is the same method of information transfer used by educators in schools. A child in the foundation level of education is taught first simple addition of sums, then subtraction, division, and multiplications. This is normally done in a progressive manner so that the child gets to understand the subject at hand before moving to the next level. If at any one time, two topics are introduced together, then there is normally total confusion on the child's part. Skipping any of these topics means that the child will lack the foundation on which to build the next. Once the addition and subtraction skills have been mastered, then division and multiplication of sums becomes easy to learn.

Before our children's sixth birthdays, we found that it was easier for them to receive toys than to share. They most likely thought that everything belonged to them, and thus, they would rather add more to what they already had. After some time, and especially following their attendance of nursery school, they learned to give away and share toys. It is probable that, if we had tried teaching them hard sharing skills at an earlier age than this, they would have become disappointed. We had to introduce the sharing skill in them by building on the free will and choice that came from within them. In order to teach them another version of giving as they grow up, there are moments when my husband and I have had to make them give or share out of mandate, not because they have chosen to do so. This is because we now know that they can handle picking one out of their nice toys and giving it away. They can choose which toy to give, but it becomes a must giving if better course has to be followed. By so doing, our children have received the message that, as parents, we would like them to draw the difference between the 'giving of free will' and the parting with one of their toys because they have to. This family rule has been slowly introduced and at a level that our children can handle. Of course, the best part of this lesson is when our children have had to learn that toys, at times, have to be given away when they are still new and straight from the toy stores.

If too little information is given to the child, then the child's understanding of the subject at hand will be incomplete. The information that every parent gives his or her child needs to be just enough for the purpose or the occasion it serves. However, it is upon every parent to take the initiative towards gaining the skills that would give him or her a command as to when to start, pause, or stop giving information. Simple information should take priority before the parent embarks on an explication of complicated issues. In the same way, it is easier for a child to follow simple house rules before he or she can cope with the rules, regulations, and policies that exist outside the home environment. This, for example, applies when it comes to teaching our children good behaviour. Good manners, like saying 'thank you' and 'excuse me' begin at home before spreading to the outside. This may seem to be an insignificant thing, but it later yields into a major thing that describes and affects the neighbourhood, the community, and the nation at large. It is unrealistic for any parents to expect their child who is not well ordered at home to take an instant turn and behave well at school or in the community. Even if such a child tries his or her level best, the reality of the matter eventually becomes clear. We must slowly teach and instil in our children the information that will help them to live respectfully, and this should be done at the appropriate opportunities. By planting the seeds of adherence to rules and regulations and slowly providing bits of nourishing information, the seeds will grow and germinate into big information. What I mean by this is that children start by understanding small bits of information before they can move to understanding a wide range of information. In another good example, the information about teenage changes cannot be fed to a five years old child. As a child grows, we should give him or her only necessary information. This is normally done at the appropriate stages of life or as the child's need or interest in topics arises. Parents need to take the lead in the distribution of information because they are, for the most part, the ones who best know their children's developmental levels. If parents take time to understand their children, then they will be able to come in first-line position of knowing the kind of information that is applicable at their child's age and how much the child can accommodate. It is important that parents watch out for and utilize any arising possible opportunity for teaching or instructing the child. When deciding what information to give to a child, when to give it, and how to deliver it, parents should bear in mind that every individual child's level of understanding greatly differs.

On the other hand, what your child learns from somewhere else or somebody else is not always harmful, so long as proper guidance and correction of misunderstandings is given. Inasmuch as people learn from mistakes, our children do not have to always learn from mistakes. All endeavours should be taken to be sure that the child is not confused regarding life issues and left in an unaided state, hanging between decisions. Just as a traveller's path should be smooth and enjoyable, so should a child's growth and development journey be calm, pleasurable, sure, and comfortable. Any connections or change over points on any journey should be clearly directional. This is why there are always signposts at bus stops, train stations, on the roads, and in other such places. A child's journey through life is just like that of a traveller, who should reach his or her final destination without having to go back to the starting point of the journey. Losing sight of one's final destination is a waste of time and discourages individuals. This most often leads to the desire to give up, delayed milestones, and other setbacks that would devastate your child.

Every child has the ability to achieve anything, as long as assistance, direction, and advice are given with wisdom, as opposed to with effort. Through encouragement, inspiration, motivation, reward, and positive comments, let the child discover his or her own self and not lose him or herself. It is best to give good direction and advice and then leave it to the child to take charge. My parents once taught me that friendship is maintained through honesty, trust, truthfulness, and kindness. These words of advice from my parents came my way when I fell off with one of my friends. I am glad that these are words that have always helped me. When I was growing up, often times my parents would remind me that I couldn't expect to get friends unless I had the above qualities and proved myself to be friendly with my siblings and people in the neighbourhood. The wide world of friendship was broken down by my parents into a level that became simple and understandable. For example, my parents laid down ground rules on how we could treat each other as siblings, how we could relate to our neighbours, and how we could handle other people, including strangers. These are regulations that have stuck with me and helped me step into school, into employment, and into marriage.

I would agree with statements like 'charity begins at home' and 'short steps make up wide steps.' That is why parents need to break up information into smaller portions that the child can understand. It is the information that the child receives from the home environment and those with whom he or she is in immediate contact that normally shape the child. Whatever is cultured in childhood normally adheres within the child. In most cases, children independently uphold the learned values anywhere, without constant parental checks, reminders, or follow-ups. Although children can be influenced by other people from outside the family, the ratio of those who refuse to be influenced is higher in those children whose parents took time to instruct them early on.

This same principle can be applied in teaching our children some skills. Parents can work alongside their children at the beginning of the subject at hand. For example, in mathematics, when working out sums, the child's self independence should be the main aim. In this way, the child will be able to work out similar sums with understanding, independently, and with fewer struggles than before. The child's own initiative and determination are the two tools he or she needs for every achievement. Too much parental involvement will confuse the child and lead to him or her losing sense of direction. Parents should assist their child as he or she takes on certain roles and responsibilities simply by being there in the case the child slips or gets stranded. Parents should avoid pestering their children. *'And you, fathers, do not provoke your children to wrath, but bring them up in the training and admonition of the Lord'* (Ephesians 6: 4).

If good distance is kept and care is taken not to reverse but to maintain the two positions of a child and a parent, then respect and trust will be earned from both sides. Instead of attempting to overcome worries and fears for our children and instead of hoping to gain control over them, parents should commit themselves to prayer in faith. *'The effective, fervent prayer of a righteous man avails much'* (James 5:16). The Creator of humankind has a better way of understanding and managing your child. He alone owns the prescription and the guidebook that can fix the areas that need amendment in your child's life. *'Be anxious for nothing, but in everything by prayer and supplication, with thanksgiving, let your request be made known to God'* (Philippians 4:6).

The maintenance of a healthy child to parent relationship can be compared to the physics behind balancing on a seesaw or a weighing machine. These two tools operate by an equilibrium mechanism that necessitates the adjustment of position in the case of a seesaw and the change of weight value in the case of a weighing machine. In assuming that both the child and the parent are of average weight and height for their ages, in order to bear one another's weight and attain a balance, the two cannot sit opposite one another at the same distance from the pivot. The application of distance alteration towards or away from the control centre and weight value changes is necessary. The farther away you move from the pivot, the more dangerously high your child gets lifted up. Taking a steady move towards the pivot gently lowers your child to a safe level. Your weight may demand that you get nearer to the pivot, but remember to stick to a balancing distance. In the case of maintaining balance on a weighing scale, it's necessary that additional weight is added on your child's side. This additional weight can be compared to nurturing the abilities and the potentials identified in your child and supplementing for any lack. The knowledge and the skills possessed by parents are part of this needed additional weight. It is good and safe to add to what your child lacks in life so that an ideal equilibrium state is eventually reached. Only in the achievement of this juncture can the two of you be happy to swing each other on any balance, the excitement of which compares to swinging on swings at the park whilst enjoying the summer sunshine. The peak of happiness and fulfilment attained at this point is what every individual would yearn for and embrace. Parenting should be characterized by bringing about this balance and maintaining this desired mutual child to parent relationship. At the age of twelve, most children are sensible and sensitive to interpreting even the slightest adjustments in relationships. The application of the method used in seesaw and weighing machine balancing means that any slight distance adjustment moves the parties in a relationship towards or away from each other; and any unnecessary additional weight means bearing each other.

Relationship balance and maintenance can only be achieved by observing certain rules that are best kept by parents. The growing child is the one who mainly gets affected because of inexperience and low tolerance ratio. All effort should be undertaken to avoid strain on the child's side, since this can prove to be detrimental. The child should not be brought to the point of finding it hard to withstand his or her parents; this leads to inability, giving up, and seeking other alternatives for comfort or advice. Keeping the picture of the seesaw balancing in mind, it may seem hard for parents, but endeavouring to stay on balance is the best option, lest the child gets dumped on the ground, especially if this occurs suddenly. At no time should a parent sit right on top of the pivot, since by so doing, he or she will ensure that the child lacks control, remains at ground level, and remains inexperienced in facing challenges. This is like asserting too much control, and it undermines the child. The distance that keeps the swing going should be wisely maintained. If you keep a far distance, your child will be discouraged and give up trying.

Some parents do acquire the habit of getting too close or too involved in monitoring or controlling the child and his or her affairs. The end result of such parental involvement leaves the child with a feeling that is similar to being squashed or suffocated. As a result, your child will be underdeveloped and irritated; he or she will kick off and revolt; and his or her vision will be killed, thwarting his or her plans, dreams, and ambitions and degrading his or her morale. When our daughter first learned how to button her school cardigan, she would never allow anyone else do it for her. Insisting on doing it for her would only result in her throwing tantrums of anger and frustration because we did not honour her request. This is how we learned that we were getting too involved in what she could do independently. Inasmuch as anyone thought that she did the buttoning incorrectly, our involvement only often left her irritated. This may sound like a small task to some people, but any toddler would easily be left feeling discouraged, incapacitated, and mistrusted if not allowed to complete it on his or her own. The effect of these feelings may progress to future giving up or overdependence on parents or adults to do things for him or her. Our little girl was determined to show us what she could also do, and we had to be careful not to kill her morale by allowing her to do it herself. She learned a do-it-yourself style and stepped into doing the next thing to show off. Since children mostly imitate adults, they only need guidance, a soft correction, and at times a cautiously delayed correction. Many times, our daughter's buttoning did not line up, but we had to find a better way of correcting it. Things would fall in proper line for correction if we first and foremost recognized what she had done, praised her, clapped for her, and sought her permission before attempting to correct the buttoning. By doing this, we taught our daughter that her individual contributions were appreciated and respected. There were occasions when we would delay the correction until her attention got distracted; then we would embark on buttoning her cardigan correctly.

Jesus had a bigger vision of becoming a teacher, and He is the greatest teacher that has ever lived. Mary and Joseph must have supported Him to grow in this. This explains why, when it comes to helping our children grow wings that they can fly on, the eagle's way of training its eaglets is the admirable, adorable and advisable pathway to copy. The eagle is normally eager to not only watch the eaglet excel but to also catch the eaglet at the sign of danger. When teaching its eaglet how to fly, it lets go of the eaglet from a height but then, in a timely fashion, reaches for it and catches it before it hits the ground. If your child takes long to catch up with what you are teaching him or her, then this eagle's way of viewing your efforts will keep you going. The eagle does not seem to get tired or give up on its eaglet, and thus should you as a parent maintain faith in your child's ability. '*But those who wait on the Lord shall renew their strength; they shall mount up with wings like eagles, they shall run and not be weary, they shall walk and not faint*' (Isaiah 40:31). During a comparative way of training your child, at the discovery that he or she can fly, parents need to know the best time to gently let go of the string attached to their child that they so tightly hold onto.

Still, every parent should remember that, while his or her child is flying in the air and keeping a good distance away, watchfulness enables the parent to rightly and necessarily step in and provide help. Parents at this point could choose to physically stand beside the child and not leave him or her, or they could psychologically support the child by using words of affirmation and reassurance. A child who knows that his or her parent is admiring, adoring, and valuing his or her flight will always come back for a hug or a handshake.

However awkward the flight may have seemed, the ability to receive the child back is what will keep the relationship going and strong. When parents readily receive their child back, they communicate to the child that they are aware the child endeavoured at his or her best level. Accidents and awkward landing situations are never absent, but just like an eaglet, your child needs picking up, comforting, and nursing. At the end of a weary journey, you should be available for consolation and to provide a shoulder for your child to lean on. In occasions of anticipated danger, your child's physical wellbeing requires your physical presence—*your* hands to grab, *your* arms to shield and protect, *your* feet to run and support, *your* eyes to watch out and guide, *your* ears to listen, *your* mouth to instruct and advise, and lastly, *your* shoulder for landing on. There are moments when our children take part in competitions and their team ends up losing or scoring fewer points. If the child has put a lot of effort into the event, the loss can be psychologically devastating to the child; all children are inclined to always want to be the winners. Parents should be first in providing the restful shoulder for a child in such a situation to lean on as he or she digests the matter. When I talk about the shoulder, I am referring to the different ways a parent can stand with their child at every challenging moment. It is the little things that build up in a child that affect his or her moral and general outlook on future life. Children need a place to offload burdens and refresh themselves so they can start all over again; and parents should be foremost in fulfilling this purpose.

However, as the child's knowledge regarding competitions increases, the child starts to notice that there are differences in the way people are rewarded for their work. It then becomes imperative for parents to take advantage of the opportunity before them and of their responsibility to assist their child through the process of learning to work hard and aiming for quality work. I know that in order to avoid discouraging children, there are times for a fair game in which everyone is a winner in the game. But this form of rewarding every participant as a winner fades or becomes limited to certain places, particular games, and different age groups. As children grow older, parents should take the responsibility of bringing to table the notion that winning and losing is part of any game and that the child or the team will be rewarded depending on the efforts put in. The earlier the child knows the reward system the better; for only with this knowledge will the child start working hard or understanding that wins and losses are part of life.

This forms a good foundation for teaching your child about greater losses that people face in life—for example the losses that result in the event of natural disasters, the loss of loved ones, or the loss of loved things. It's also a good idea to seize this opportunity and give instructions regarding the practical day-to-day challenges that contribute to differences in individual lives. This is when the parent builds the steps for the child to climb onto as he or she faces life challenges and hurdles. When a child understands the nature of losing and winning, he or she will be persuaded to work hard and with great dedication for the things that he or she desires. Consider, for example, what may result if a child goes out to play and badly falls off with his or her playmates. A phobia of going outdoors to play could set in, or the child may learn to carry on, leading to recurrent disagreements with his or her friends. Parents, at this point, need to teach their children conflict resolution skills, starting in the home environment before the lack of such skills spreads into the community.

In sorting out some issues, parental reassurance and guidance will be of vital aid. The child's way of handling future issues depends greatly on childhood experiences, and for this reason, no caring parent should allow his or her child to carry bad experiences into the future. The child should be assisted in developing a habit of offloading, outgrowing, and reversing bad experiences and obstacles for a better tomorrow. Your ability to timely identify when your child needs this help is what will give you the eagle's eyesight. An eagle can spot things from afar, and, thus, parents who are like the eagle parents are those who perceive their children's needs in a timely fashion. The ability of the eagle parent to see its eaglet flourish and excel is what gives it the power that it symbolizes. Likewise, parents can attain this eagle power by seeing to it that their children flourish and excel. The transitional journey from childhood into the teenage years can be scary, intimidating, and wearisome, but parents can be the source of reassurance. When the transition is safely done, the benefit, the advantage, and the profit will be for the good of both the child and the parent, but helping the child rise to the next level of life should comprise the whole purpose of parenting.

By the time the child turns twelve, most of what he or she has become and achieved is normally a result of the parents' contributions and influences. This is mainly because children before the age of twelve easily and trustingly do what they are asked to do, with little if any questioning or resistance. This is the stage in a child's life wherein the power and authority of the parent is fully seen. Unless in compromised relationships, most children, before their teenage years, only know their parents to be big, strong, experienced, and the best. Knowing this, children fully trust their parents and feel secure whilst they are with their parents. However, do not forget that, as the child approaches the age of twelve, influences from the outside world do set in and are likely to affect the child's view of the home environment. Depending on the effect of these influences, your experimental child may eventually start challenging your beliefs and questioning your regulations. With the child's demonstration of his or her developing independence and decision-making ability comes the liability that he or she will want to deviate from your values and traditions. This independence and decision-making ability is totally opposed to what most parents conclude or label as 'disobedience.' If values and traditions are well explained beforehand and their meanings are clearly drawn out, children will, in most cases, prove to be more cooperative than we think. Most parents conclude that the child is disobedient when they have not taken time to clarify things to the child. Although parents have authority, they should refrain from imposing their ideas on the child and seek to clarify things. If a parent takes time to understand the child, then the child is unlikely to question the values and the traditions the parents have established. You can maintain good communication skills with your child by working together whilst explaining and clarifying things. This will draw the two of you towards a mutual understanding.

You should dispose of any form of relationship that suggests controlling or interfering in the affairs of your child. This interfering behaviour only leads to reversion, resistance, and a strained child-parent relationship. If the required trust is part of a well-laid foundation, most of the clashing issues that arise at this age will be eliminated. The focus and concentration at this stage in life should be strengthening what you've already instilled in the child. It is difficult, even unrealistic, to start introducing sudden new rules and regulations in an older child. This child may not understand the need for such sudden and new changes, and eventually it is you, the parent, who will be upset. The simplest things, like setting a bedtime when your child is still young, are important. If you don't set restrictions early in life, your child may develop the tendency to stay awake

Sophia William

till late; and he or she will have difficulty getting out of such a habit. Another example is setting a time limit for staying out. Parents should have a time limit when it comes to how late their children can stay out and how far from home they can go. If given freedom or if this is not checked, children tend to think that they can stay out as late as they want and that they can go as far away from home as they wish. This routine is likely to get worse as the child grows, and it will be much harder to introduce regulations to a child who experienced no set limits at an early age. Preteen children tend to get quite absorbed in social life, and as such, parents need to set rules regarding the time when they should return home, since they cannot stay out as long as they want.

Children need to be taught and instructed when it comes to self-control and patience, especially before going out for meetings like attending church, it is always good to talk to your children about the need to maintain silence and avoid disturbing others. Although children are prone to forget or be naughty, mainly when they want to catch your attention, parent's effort in instructing finally takes root. Teach your child that he or she needs to have a timetable and a study time in order to improve his or her grades. Children and parents need to agree upon and set rules regarding homework and submission of school assignments. If your child does not learn to be self-disciplined, set priorities, and value his or her homework, he or she will surely have problems with discipline in future.

There should be set relational morals in every family. For example, when it comes to relating with siblings and other people, no one in the family should be permitted to swear or shout at each other if this falls out of the family norms. As early as possible and as it is appropriate, children should be taught about personal hygiene, as well as; the need to tidy up their rooms, make their beds, arrange their books, keep their toys picked up, tidy their wardrobes, and the like. It is only from these small tasks that your child will learn how to handle bigger household tasks or gain organization skills.

We must pray and trust that the good values we have instilled in our children will not follow the adage, 'It is easier to dismantle than to construct.' As long as the return of Christ Jesus tarries, parents, through faith, should keep holding on, '*being confident of this very thing, that He who has begun a good work in you will complete it until the day of Jesus Christ*' (Philippians 1:6). In the hands of a farmer, the eggs laid by a hen become precious, but the hen itself still remains valuable. In the hands of a parent, the foundation that has already been laid for the child and the child himself or herself form two preciously valued and inseparable things. The farmer takes good care of the hen and at the same time knows how to handle, pack, store, and transport the eggs from the farm to the consumer. The farmer learns how to handle and protect the eggs from adverse conditions like extreme temperatures and humidity. These are some of the conditions that could spoil the eggs. In the same way, it is upon the parent to learn and know each individual child and prepare him or her for the life ahead. In order that the child is able withstand the world's influences that may prove detrimental to his or her growth and development, the parent is obliged to ensure that the child is prepared, protected, and cautioned. As a child transitions from childhood to adulthood, it is vital for the parent to know what the child can handle and how much input in the form of support is required. The farmer knows the fragility of an egg and adopts special ways of handling it. In the same way, parents must be careful when dealing with their preteen child.

This child has a delicacy that compares to that of an egg. The oval shape, as opposed to the supposedly circular shape, of an egg gives it two visionary shapes that interrelate to the two dimensioned stage of life that a preteen child reaches.

At the age of twelve, the child is bombarded with decisions that seem to have two options to choose from. These decisions also seem to characteristically fall at the verge of a 'start' and an 'end'. The struggle between these verges calls for parental guidance. It is only with guidance that the child is able to make informed, good, and solid decision. In most children, an internal war develops when it comes to making these decisions. There is the struggle between following their parents' or their friends' ideas. There is the struggle as to whether to continue with the traditions of the home environment or approve the influences from the outside world. Every parent anticipates that his or her child will adhere to parental guidance and avoid the influences that draw children away from good home relations and regulations. This is because inasmuch as different parents may have different rules, every parent aims to set rules that are for the child's benefit. It is also apparent that most parents bring up their children based on the experiences that they have gone through. They mainly aim to shield their child from the bad experiences that they themselves underwent. They thrive to bring up the child in the best way that they discovered along their life journey. The home environment may not accept things like late parties, smoking, alcohol, swearing, fighting, and the like, whilst the child's friends may be influencing the child toward these things. One phase unfolds into the present and the future, and the other phase folds into the past milestones.

If the child is to enjoy and fulfil his or her future, then the childhood to adulthood transition demands present, wise, and intact decisions from parents and other adults in the child's life. Remember that an intact egg has a longer market period than a broken egg; and a broken egg has a limited usage period that demands quicker consummation and yet giving less profit. An egg is oval rather than circle, and understanding your child's phase of life may not be as straightforward as you may think, but both eggs and your child require tenderness in handling.

Individual children reach the stage at which they are able to do or understand certain things at different ages, and defining those stages is difficult with every child. Not being able to demarcate the developmental phases of your child makes it hard to handle your tender child, just as an egg is delicate to handle. Yet if properly done, handling both eggs and children is easy.

Consider driving around a roundabout that is round like a ball versus driving around one that is oval like an egg. Navigating the ball-shaped path will be much easier than navigating the oval-shaped one. The skill required to navigate both trails is the same, but the second requires that the driver apply more caution. Parenting preteens can be compared to driving along an oval-shaped roundabout; precautionary measures are necessary when it comes to manoeuvring.

Every child has individual choices and preferences, and no one can claim that they have fully comprehended the child's exact level or stage. Every child considerably differs in his or her pattern of growth and development, and this cannot be completely described, just as an egg is not wholly circular. The preteen stage is delicate to handle, but if parents deal with this stage well, the child will likely pass through the teen years and arrive at adulthood well. The main aim is a decent transition from childhood into adulthood; for only then will the parental responsibility form a fitting foundation. The pointed end of an egg is its strong part, to which you can apply pressure, but its flattened end is its weakest part, and you should avoid applying pressure there. Parents should know the obvious sensitive areas in the child's life and handle this at the child's individual level but with caution. For example, you may notice that your child, whom you still consider to be young, has started picking up some habits that are likely to result from influences from friends; it is your parental responsibility to disapprove of such friends but in a way that makes the child understand the importance of building healthy relations. For example, you shouldn't embarrass your child by screaming at him or her and dragging him or her from such friendship, but instead you should find a better way of talking to your child in order to instil in him or her the importance of good choices. During the preteen years, the child starts to yearn for independence and respect from his or her parents, but parents should remember that they still need to caressingly guard the life of this child.

The slightly long-ended and stretched sides of an egg are indicative of an existing degree of stretch within its shell. In the same way, there is already an existing degree of stretch within your child as he or she decides between life options. The child gets mixed feelings that come along with adapting to what the parent has to offer and making his or her own decisions. It is the parent's responsibility to make sure that the child makes informed decisions and is not stretched further or unreasonably compressed with the various influences, changes, and choices that he or she faces. In terms of fragility, every parent or guardian is called upon to differentiate between the child's favourable side that can be safely touched and the unfavourable side that should be exclusively left in the child's capacity. Compressing the two ends of an eggshell reveals its strength, which forms the packaging support. Compressing its flat side reveals its weakness, accounting for its delicacy. Likewise, your child has strong and weak areas, and inasmuch as it is vital to discover and harness the child's strengths, knowing any areas of weaknesses prevents breakages.

In most cases, children can be naturally fearful, weak in emotions, poor in facing confrontations, unable to solve complex problems, and may lack concentration, but it is the responsibility of the parent to form the first source of reassurance and support in this case. Lack of coping ability in this case may extremely drag the child into awkward versions of handling stressful situations. A parent who perceives the above awkward reaction in their child should solve the matter early enough before it gets out of control. For example, if a child displays severe anger outbursts, an underlying reason for the behaviour may be in existence. Parents who cannot manage to resolve this should seek other available sources of help, such as counselling services. All the packaging materials for transporting eggs should give adequate breathing space, allowing oxygen to circulate. Similarly, you should avoid pressurizing your child, so as to provide some breathing space and freedom.

An egg carries the life of a chick, which later hatches and grows into a mature hen or cock. Relatively, as your child passes from childhood into adulthood, his or her potentials need to mature. You can never create angles or corners on an egg unless you have an intention of breaking it. However, you can improve or change its outward appearance by gently painting or decorating it. Comparatively, at the child's advanced age, shaping up, polishing up, and adding to what your child already possesses is more profitable and less harmful than trying to make changes. In the same way, parents must be careful when it comes to recognizing their children's capabilities and working towards improvement, enhancement, growth, and establishment of the values already found in each child.

There are many areas in which parents can help their children work towards growth and improvement. Parents can recognize their child's abilities. For example, if you notice that your child is good at sports; talented at singing; or does well in computer skills, arithmetic, literature, art, cookery, or any other skill, the best thing you can do is nurture these abilities, talents, and gifts. This could take the form of encouraging your child, paying tuition and fees to enrol him or her in extra lessons, attending your child's performances, and congratulating him or her. Human beings enjoy being recognized, and by noticing and appreciating your children's effort, you help them find value in what they are doing, so they will continue honing and practicing their skills into the future and will gain the benefits of doing so.

In schools, teachers are good at recognizing the abilities and talents of the children who are under their care, but parents need to stand up and take part in this also. Remember that it is not just enough to recognize the child's strengths; it's necessary to go the extra mile of supporting the child. This comes into practice, for example, when the parent takes time off to spend with the child as he or she works on the area of talent.

Parents should be aware of children who are susceptible to the desire to live in a comfort zone. A child can easily pick up unhealthy lifestyle behaviours. An example of this is a child who would rather sit and watch the television for long hours but refuse to spare time for his or her homework or for undertaking a physical exercise. Parents need to realise that such a child needs prompting to change activities, assistance with time management, and provision of other available recreational activities. The root cause of this unhealthy lifestyle can be eradicated if dealt with early in life, but it calls for parental guidance, involvement, and planning with the child.

As the child grows physically, he or she must be growing mentally and gaining maturity as well; if not, then treatment or advice should be sought. As the child grows, he or she needs to start mimicking adulthood behaviours. For example, children should learn simple household tasks like attending to personal and environmental hygiene needs, washing dishes, doing laundry, folding clothes, tidying the house, preparing a cup of tea, toasting bread, preparing a snack, and the like. Parents should also teach their children how to cope with a wide range of issues, including how to budget, manage time, relate with others, resolve conflicts, manage money, and deal with body growth and changes.

When it comes to academic studies, children need to mentally shift from elementary education standards and graduate to high school level of education. The quantity and quality of work that the child produces at primary school level should differ and improve as the child progresses at high school level. Thus, parents ought to prepare their child early enough and make the child aware that extra academic effort will be required. If parents ensure that this is done gradually, then abrupt changes or adjustments will be avoided. For example, parents should take the lead when the child needs to improve upon his or her school work. Good grades build confidence, and parents can enable this through support and encouragement at home, liaising with the child's teachers, paying for extra tutorials and helping the child to work around a timetable.

In the case of money management, advise the child against luxurious expenditures, especially when it comes to spending their dinner money at school. As the child approaches his or her preteen, parents should talk to him or her about the physical body changes that come with adolescence. For example, parents should take time to inform the child of the positive and negative effects of these changes in regards to hygiene, dressing, behaviour, relationships, and the like. At this stage, parents should aim to link the child's growth and developmental changes with the child's knowledge by giving meaningful and timely training and direction.

The child steps into a new realm of social, academic, spiritual, psychological, physical, economical, and emotional challenges. These factors may prove incomprehensible, but they are important and unavoidable. The pace at which children are introduced to these challenges may seem outrageous, and this may seem to cause a rampage within your child, but it is to the child's advantage if he or she learns how to face, handle, and cope with these factors and their accompanying changes. However, being aware of the individual child's pace and ability to cope is more important. Where possible, it is wiser to limit parental involvement and emphasize developing, enabling, and empowering the child's own initiative. As your child grows older, only measurable and reasonable parental participation is necessary to reinforce a positive outlook of life and build his or her confidence. The influences and the contributions that result from your child interacting with other people and friends are necessary, but the parent's availability, guidance, wise counsel, and support will assist the child in developing healthy relationships and making the right choices.

Shutting your child in the closet of the home environment is unhealthy and contradictory to the freedom that your child needs in order to explore and safely unveil the world. Interacting with your child is better than interfering with his or her affairs. As children grow and develop mentally, there will be moments when they may want to do their own things, for example keeping in touch with friends. Parents should come to a common ground of agreement on what can be done and what cannot be done through collaboration with the child but keep in mind that the child's health and safety is paramount. As children grow and approach the preteen years, their interest in socializing increases, they may want to keep in touch with their friends through emails, text messages, or social networking. A parent who decides to cut off a child's communications with his or her friends is interfering instead of interacting. If, however, the parent guides the child as to the kind of friends he or she should keep, the things that are appropriate to discuss, the places he or she may go to, the amount of time he or she should spend with friends, this eventually becomes interaction. In interaction, the parties involved seek and reach a common line of agreement, but in interference, one party is deprived of freedom and rights.

However, the misuse of these privileges, established through interaction on the child's part, is dangerous, and the parent who notices this and fails to warn the child is acting ignorantly. If a child fails to change while he or she is still young, he or she may not change in the future. For example, if parents find out that their child is spending a lot of time on the phone, the best approach is to softly talk to the child about time management or limit his or her allowances on telephone use, rather than demanding that the child should stop keeping in touch with his or her friends altogether.

Parents should also take on the duty of introducing things to, rather than imposing them on, their children. For example, if you would like your child to accomplish a household task that is not routine, it is good to tell your child in advance so that he or she does not miss out on appointments made with his or her friends. If you place your demands on your child's plans, he or she may interpret this as intruding. Your children should also be certain in the knowledge that you will always love them and be available to them. Offering yourself when needed is the best gift that you can ever give your child, but appearing behind or before your child when not invited will offend your child, and he or she will classify this as meddlesome behaviour. The parental role of teaching and mentoring should be principled and coincide with an environment that is conducive to ensuring that children don't shy away or get put off. Instead, the child should be able to confide in and have confidence in his or her parents.

# 2

## Education before the Child's Twelfth Birthday

In many parts of the world, primary school education for every child has been adopted and made a compulsory requirement. Parents can be penalized for keeping their children from school or get cautioned for excusing excessive absences. In most education systems, the target age for finishing primary schooling revolves around the child's twelfth birthday. The acquisition of elementary education is important mainly because foundational academic strategies begin at primary learning. Secondary school education curriculum builds on the basics that have already been laid at the primary level. The linkage between these two levels of primary and secondary education helps in forming and holding the progressive blocks for future learning and achievements.

Inasmuch as most children find the move from primary school to high school exciting, the opposite effects of fear, anxiety, and challenge could easily set in and pose coping difficulties. This is why parents and teachers do their best to prepare and guide children for this challenging choice ahead. These two parties are happy when children gain self-confidence, work hard, show determination, and feel prepared to face the outside world. The child, the parents, and the teachers look forward to best future achievements and moves.

The obsession with the process of searching and selecting the type of secondary school that the child moves to next highly kicks in. Depending on parents' preferences, the move may be to a private or a public school, but the child's welfare comes first. There is basic consultation and agreement between the child and the parents regarding the chosen school. Inasmuch as the child is imparted with the skills and the attributes necessary for a successful transition from primary to secondary school, the progress made in schooling requires the child's own interest. Involving the child in choosing the school that he or she moves to is a sign of respecting the child's participation in his or her own circumstances. Considerations when making a decision about schools include the prospective schools' performance results, good behaviour records, range of facilities, and access to good and modern equipments; the travelling distance; the safety of commuting to and from school; and reports about the surrounding neighbourhood.

Schools maintain an environment of set rules, regulations, policies, and boundaries designed to meet every child's efforts and interests. In encouraging broad fulfilment of academic and social life potentials, most parents endeavour to put effort and interest in their child's progress. However, inasmuch as it is important to concentrate on your child's academic requirements, this alone is not enough to ensure that he or she succeeds at school; nor is it all that your child needs for life. It is, therefore, essential that parents shift from a one-dimensional focus and adapt to a well-rounded view of their child's life.

Governments and schools are two forms of institutions with operational systems. In both, there are rules, regulations, policies, and boundaries to keep and observe. In the same way, it is good to realize that every home is an institution with its individualized and esteemed values. These values form unique family customs and are safeguarded by rules, regulations, policies, and boundaries. If these safe and good traditions are kept functional, then they later propagate into the next generation. If the teaching and the instilling of the esteemed family values is done at the earliest possible opportunity and if these values positively contribute towards the child's future; then they are worth bringing to reality and being spread. This compares to the upbringing of Jesus. '*His parents went to Jerusalem every year at the Feast of the Passover. And when He was twelve years old, they went up to Jerusalem according to the custom of the feast*' (Luke 2:41-42).

# 3

## Mary and Joseph before their Child's Twelfth Birthday

Mary and Joseph exemplified the beauty of a godly parenting that can be spoken of, supported, and demonstrated today. We can arrive at this conclusion when we examine the excellence of their ability to get every member of the family to adhere to God's law and regulations. They went to Jerusalem every year to celebrate the Passover feast. They performed the parental duty of taking their child with them. Children are disadvantaged when parents neglect and fail to comply with and perform certain parental duties.

Mary and Joseph's parenting offers a recorded example to be upheld and copied by present day parents. In their example, we clearly see that those parents who would like to pass on valuable, fundamental, and compulsory foundational practices are better off if they start doing so at the child's earliest age. The direction taken by Jesus exemplifies how children esteem and emulate their parents' actions. This further demonstrates that the values our children follow and uphold are best founded before the age of twelve. In examining Mary and Joseph's family, we can gain an understanding of the style of parenting we should pass on for generations. Guided by his earthly parents, Jesus grew up and perpetuated the lessons Mary and Joseph taught him. '*But when Jesus saw it, He was greatly displeased and said to them, "Let the little children to come to Me, and do not forbid them; for of such is the kingdom of God"'* (Mark 10:14). Mary and Joseph taught their child and spent time with him when he was very young, and he followed their example. At the age of twelve and before, a child is tenderly recipient, prone to be dependent, inclined to trust, and able to copy. It is generally easy to get children of this age to be obedient, and they are minimally resistant to their parents. After this age, children grow into a state of independence and become choice orientated and opinionated. It is common for children to start challenging their parent's ideas, opinions, and choices. But the evolved customary practices that form the individualized family traditions are mostly considered by parents to be inherent. That is why, for the most part, whatever parents uphold becomes part and parcel of their growing child's lifestyle and mostly for the generations that follow.

It is never too late for those parents who have missed out on proper parenting. They should start immediately, instead of regretting over what's in the past. Jesus says, '*Let the little children to come to Me, and do not forbid them; for of such is the kingdom of God*' (Mark 10:14b). Responsibility is thus laid upon parents when it comes to getting children to their maker. '*So then faith comes by hearing, and hearing by the word of God*' (Romans 10:17). If our children hear the Word of God, faith will be created in them. Parents are happy to see their children excel in academics and extracurricular activities; it is not fair for parents to actively deny their children the chance to tap into the knowledge of the creator of humanity. Our children graduate from schools, achieve grades, and win medals, and hindering these children from access to the things of the kingdom of God is improper. The crown of life awaits to be won and aspired for by us, together with our children. In a similar situation of urging people to make informed decisions, Joshua addressed the children of Israel by saying, '*And if it seems evil to you to serve the Lord, choose for yourselves this day whom you will serve, whether the gods which your fathers served that were on the other side of the River, or the gods of the Amorites, in whose land you dwell. But as for me and my house, we will serve the Lord*' (Joshua 24:15). There are three areas in every child's life—the body, the soul, and the spirit—and they all need nurturing. An empty space is susceptible to be occupied by anything that comes in; thus it is of paramount importance that parents strive to appropriately occupy the child in all the three areas. There are many things that we can occupy our children with, but maintaining a good and a proper balance of what we engage our children in is important. For those parents who have their Christian faith to uphold, there should be no reason to shy away from taking their children to the house of God. The problems of present day parenting dilemmas can be solved by counting Mary and Joseph as heroes of the parenting world and emulating their parenting style. If our children end up loving the house of God the way Jesus did, then they should be encouraged to do so. There is a reward awaiting our children for this act, just as they are rewarded for good performance in schools, at places of employment, and the like. The act of faith that involves taking our children to the house of God and teaching them biblical values may seem simple or irrelevant to the majority in our communities, but it taps in divine blessings. There is no parent who would refuse blessings for their child.

Mary and Joseph took Jesus to the temple to present Him to God. They understood the significance of this and took action. '*Now when the days of her purification according to the law of Moses were completed, they brought Him to Jerusalem to present Him to the Lord*' (Luke 2:22). We can confirm from the words of Simeon and Anna that there is a definite flow of blessings, revelations, and confirmations that follow this practice. (Read Luke 2:21-38.) There are many things about our children that only God knows. Mary and Joseph had already received a lot of witness regarding their child's uniqueness. '*And all those who heard it marvelled at those things which were told them by the shepherds*' (Luke 2:18). But when they brought the child to the temple on this day, they still marvelled at what they heard. '*And Joseph and His mother marvelled at those things that were spoken of Him*' (Luke 2:33). This teaches all parents that what we know about our children is only but limited until we bring them to the house of God, where more is exposed to us.

Did you know that there is an excellent way to bring up your child? Whatever your answer may be, I am about to share with you the best way ever recorded to bring up your growing child. In this era of life, there once lived a couple who brought up their child in an admirable, successful, and excellent way. Their achievement is measured by the way they brought up their boy from childhood into responsible adulthood. The example their child set, the fame accorded to Him, and the impact He made on the world still remain to be considered exceptional. The boy was Jesus, who first spoke publicly when He was twelve years old and resurfaced in His adulthood. What can we learn from His parents? Did His parents play any part in His final outcome, or did He become only what God had predestined? God works through people, and that is why Jesus needed parents. Every child needs parenting, and that is why Jesus needed parents. If God didn't work through people, He might just as well have supernaturally dropped Jesus into the world without giving Him parents.

Great debate may arise at this point, but Mary and Joseph have already dictated the best way of parenting, and this holds you indebted. If you think that it was easy for them and that their parental example is too ancient for me to be talking about, I would urge you to think of anyone else who has ever coped with the circumstances that surrounded them and their child. "*Behold, the virgin shall be with child and bear a Son, and they shall call His name Immanuel," which is translated, "God with us*'" (Matthew 1:23). Doubts do also arise in people who have already heard and read of Jesus. This then confirms that the speculations and the rumours around the above message of conception must have been great indeed. Even after reading about the miraculous works of God in the Bible, some people still doubt. Jesus' parents fought against the odds and the forces that faced them and their child.

I imagine that Jesus' age mates made jokes about what they had heard of Him and His parents. In the present world, both children and adults make jokes or mock each other. Great things had been spoken about Jesus, and yet He was only from a humble family and without any physical traits to distinguish Him from other children around Him. He too was faced with challenges, just like His parents, and yet He was only a child who needed support. This support must have only come from His parents and a few others, such as Auntie Elizabeth, Uncle Zachariah, and Cousin John.

If King Herod was not happy about this child, then the majority followed. '*When Herod the king heard this, he was troubled, and all Jerusalem with him*' (Matthew 2:3). Baby Jesus had to be shielded from the evil intentions of Herod the king. '*Then Herod, when he had secretly called the wise men, determined from them what time the star appeared*' (Matthew 2:7). But these wise men from the East were divinely warned in a dream to depart for their own country using another way.

Joseph received a similar warning in a dream. '*Arise, take the young Child and His mother, flee to Egypt, and stay there until I bring you word; for Herod will seek the young Child to destroy Him*' (Matthew 2:13b). This was only the beginning of the challenges that Jesus and His parents were to face, but His parents must have dedicated themselves to defending what they believed until their beliefs were brought to light. They must have supported their child in overcoming what He heard from those around Him. He was only young and growing like any other child. Jesus took the very form of humanity, and as such, He must have felt how people feel when excluded from others for one reason or another. The support of His parents, who understood Him better and believed what God had spoken about Him, was paramount. He was meant to grow up like any other child, but the odds that surrounded His birth demanded extra support and explanations to the common man. It is almost certain that people speculated and spread rumours concerning Him. It is common even in the present times for people to quickly pick out 'odd' things in others and exclude people who seem 'unordinary' in one way or another.

Before other people understood Jesus, He must have gone through the stages of understanding Himself first. Before Jesus found a voice to speak for Himself, His parents must have spoken for Him. His parents must have also aided Him in finding His identity and recognizing His significant potentials. Therefore, in this present and rewarding world that seeks for best parenting, Mary and Joseph deserve the best parent award and stand unchallenged. They knew how to nurture their child's vision and guarded it into maturity—until God turned it into a mission. They wholeheartedly devoted themselves to the formation of the good and lasting foundation that the child's future is built upon. Their child's transition from childhood into adulthood was a success. This is as per what transpired of Him at the age of twelve—the age that marks the stepping into teenage and adulthood changes. Jesus' success means that his parents succeeded too. It is said that, 'Behind every successful woman there is a man, and behind every successful man there is a woman.' It would be right to simply say that behind every successful child there are parents.

The excellence with which I credit these two parents does not deny other parents their chance of choosing the superstar, superhero, celebrity, or other role model preferable for their child's emulation. The choice depends on one's individual value system. However, among various choices, there is always the proven best way. The excellence of our choices counts when we settle for what holds the best quality and the highest efficiency.

History absolutely proves and brings up the certainty that no other character can outbalance Jesus. Jesus is the greatest teacher; He is the Son of God; He is God in the human form; He never sinned; He died for humanity; He is alive and risen from the dead; He is the way; He is the truth; He is the life; He is the bread of life; He is the living water; He is the Prince of Peace; He is the Lord of Lords; He is the King of Kings; He is the wonderful Counsellor. In reality, He is all that we need for life, and it would only be right to say that no other parenting would outwit His upbringing.

'*For in Him we live and move and have our being . . .*' (Acts 17:28). The whole topic may be given to what we have decided to choose as opposed to debate. '*Train up a child in the way he should go, And when he is old he will not depart from it*' (Proverbs 22:6). The above verse speaks of 'when he is old', meaning that the child's future depends upon the present.

On the other hand, God is interested in the present, the future, and the eternity of your child. The childhood and teenage phases have been categorized by particular age ranges, but adulthood has no age limit. Since only God knows the length of adulthood, parents should do what they can in training the child, and then one day, at God's appointed time, the given training will take root.

When Jesus was crucified at Calvary, two criminals were hanged on the cross besides Him. One of these men mocked Jesus, but the other one did not. The man who did not mock Jesus spoke respectful words and posed a question to the disrespectful one: '*Do you not even fear God, seeing you are under the same condemnation?*' (Luke 23:40b). Parents who think that there is nothing that they can do to help their child can find encouragement in the example set by this malefactor. Although he was condemned and sentenced to face the most shameful death, he recognized that he could not blaspheme Jesus. The respectful words that this malefactor spoke could have resulted from the training that he received in childhood. On his last day of being alive, he asked for what he most needed: '*Lord, remember me when You come into Your kingdom*' (Luke 23:42). His request was immediately granted when Jesus said, '*Assuredly, I say to you, today you will be with Me in paradise.*' (Luke 23:43). This gives hope to every parent who may be overwhelmed and tempted to give up on his or her child.

As long as your child is still alive, there is room for change. '*He who continually goes forth weeping, bearing seed for sowing, shall doubtless come again with rejoicing, bringing his sheaves with him*' (Psalms 126:6). The period of time when a child can be trained by his or her parents seems to be limited to the age before twelve. Thereafter, a child's lifestyle is normally shaped by whatever he or she has already acquired. Parents should not, however, cease mentioning their children to God, who is their Maker. This may sound funny, but it is like servicing your child's life. The more you ignore the commandment to speak to God on your child's behalf, at the same time correcting him or her, the more you incur damage and hurt, just as the more you neglect to have your car serviced, the more your car is damaged. Unlike cars, your child's life cannot be exchanged, and thus, ensuring that your child receives proper check-ups from his or her Maker is imperative!

'*For these things I weep; my eye, my eye overflows with water; because the comforter, who should restore my life, is far from me. My children are desolate because the enemy prevailed*' (Lamentations 1:16). Understanding what is going on within our children may seem difficult, but when things go wrong, parents should double their efforts and try out new means of reversing the situation. As the challenges intensify, then arising and taking action becomes pivotal. There will be a change in one's emotional state. '*Arise cry out in the night, at the beginning of the watches; pour out your heart like water before the face of the Lord. Lift your hands toward Him, for the life of your young children, who faint from hunger at the head of every street*' (Lamentation 2:19). The above doubling of the *chapters*, from *(1)* to *(2),* signifies strengthened efforts. The reversing of the numbers *(6)* to *(9)* in the above two *verses* means standing up and facing the situation. The shape of the number *six (6)* suggestively assumes a sitting posture which is indicative of an individual who decides to bury the head in the ground and pretend that nothing is happening. The number shape of the *nine (9)* suggestively assumes a standing position that sticks its head out and deals with the situation at hand. Parents should not refrain from correcting or dealing with any unwanted habits in their children. The urgency of stepping out and seeking parental help should not be delayed or underestimated.

If our heads remain buried in the ground and we pretend that nothing is happening, then we are failing greatly. We should stick our heads out and face reality. Only then will we move across the situations in the above two verses effectively. The good thing is that God has all the power that can stop the enemy from prevailing. Once the child starts to make his or her own decisions, parents can only give guidance around what the child already knows. Parents are called upon to pray, an act that bears fruits far into the future and is never in vain. '*Weeping may endure for a night, but joy comes in the morning*' (Psalms 30:5b)

If we admire, love, and esteem the Lordship of Jesus Christ, then our children's childhoods should be transformed by the childhood of Jesus. Only then can we discover, uphold, and treasure the truth that lies behind the success of Mary and Joseph. The Lord Jesus Christ calls on us to make some application when He asks the question, '*What then is this that is written: "The stone which the builders rejected Has become the chief cornerstone?"*' (Luke 20:17). If we include the chief cornerstone in the foundation on which we build the principles that guide our parenting and our children's lives, then we are moving toward, rather than shying away from, the best of choices.

Mary and Joseph adopted no style of parenting other than the one recorded in Luke: '*So when they had performed all things according to the law of the Lord, they returned to Galilee, to their own city, Nazareth. And the Child grew and became strong in spirit, filled with wisdom; and the grace of God was upon Him.*' (Luke 2:39-40). There are two noticeable phrases. First, Mary and Joseph '*performed all*'; they provided all that was necessary for the child's growth and development. Second, they did so '*according to the law of the Lord*'; they relied on God's instructions. The above Bible quotation contains two distinctive parts that both imply and evaluate Mary and Joseph's value system. In all their endeavours, they relied on the law of God as a guide. They valued their child, they valued the belief system instilled in their child, they valued God the giver of their child, and they valued the effect their lives had on their child and eventually on those to follow Him. This child had been given as a gift to the world, and they were to care for this gift. Their parental tasks included receiving the gift, appreciating the gift giver, and presenting the gift to humanity.

The best way to maintain your car is to follow the manufacturer's instructions. This same principle is applicable when it comes to your child's upbringing. It is important to follow the instructions of the child's Maker—the Word of God. In the case that you miss out on any step or instruction, there is no harm in perusing the pages again. When Jesus went missing, his parents went back to look for Him. This seeking for their lost child can be likened to seeking for the lost truth of parenting. When it comes to ideal parenting, the truth the world is searching for can be found in Jesus. If we do not apply Jesus' childhood to our children's milestones, they will miss out on blessings. Jesus said, '*I am the way, the truth, and the life. No one comes to the Father except through Me*' (John 14:6). If parents apply and adhere to Mary and Joseph's parenting style, then we will never miss out on the blessings that we seek for our children.

# 4

## Jesus before His Twelfth Birthday

The Lord Jesus Christ is the very example of the life that humankind should live, *'for in Him we live and move and have our being . . .'* (Acts 17:28). He is the very Word of God. *'And the Word became flesh and dwelt among us, and we beheld His glory, the glory as of the only begotten of the Father, full of grace and truth'* (John 1:14). He is the one who can perfect our ways and give purposeful living to us and our children too. *'The law of the Lord is perfect, converting the soul; the testimony of the Lord is sure, making wise the simple'* (Psalms 19:7). His parents still found it necessary to bring up Him up in accordance with this perfect law. *'The statues of the Lord are right, rejoicing the heart; the commandment of the Lord is pure, enlightening the eyes'* (Psalms 19:8). The law of God was still an essential requirement in His upbringing.

The childhood of Jesus has been laid before us as an example, and this is a pattern that is meant to remain unchanged because *'Jesus Christ is the same yesterday, today, and forever'* (Hebrews 13:8). If the very life that we live is the Lord Jesus Christ Himself, then the law of God remains a necessity in our lives and in the lives of our children. *'But the word of the Lord endures forever'* (1 Peter 1:25). Jesus has not changed at all, and his childhood has not changed either. The Word of God, by which Jesus was brought up, has not changed, and it will never pass away. '*Heaven and earth will pass away, but My words will by no means pass away*' (Matthew 24:35). The Bible has already confirmed that the impact of our Lord Jesus Christ is eternal. '*Therefore He is also able to save to the uttermost those who come to God through Him, since He always lives to make intercession for them*' (Hebrews 7:25). The child Jesus grew up in this world, just like your child, and He is ever present to help your child. He grew up just like your child, and yet He is the Lord, the Saviour, and the King that we currently know. '*I will not leave you orphans; I will come to you*' (John 14:18). Those who look unto Him shine and understand the meaning of life because He lights their path. '*Your Word is a lamp to my feet and a light to my path*' (Psalms 119: 105).

Humankind is subject to being effected by nature and the challenges that come along in life. During His walk here on the earth and in His childhood, Jesus experienced the way the world operates its systems just as any child does. His parents paid taxes; they participated in the census; attended worship services, weddings, and social gatherings; and otherwise participated in daily life. Jesus Himself socialised with people, had friends, travelled, and passed through the natural developmental stages just like any other child in those days. The most important part of this comparison is that there is great relief and reassurance in simply knowing that Jesus overcame childhood and prevailed. He has not changed, and those who follow after His example will also realize this victory. He overcame the confines of childhood, growing into perfect maturity, mentally, emotionally, and spiritually. It is written of Him, "*I am the Alpha and the Omega, the*

*Beginning and the End,"* says the Lord, *"who is and who was and who is to come, the Almighty."* (Revelation 1:8).

Whatever we can perceive from the childhood of Jesus needs to open up our minds. Whatever we can see in His childhood needs to open up our eyes. Whatever we can hear about His childhood needs to open up our ears. Whatever we read and record about the His childhood needs to open up our thoughts. As our children grow, we do not yet know what they will become, *'For we walk by faith, not by sight'* (2 Corinthians 5:7). But most of the time, parents do hope for the best things for their children. *'Now faith is the substance of things hoped for, the evidence of things not seen'* (Hebrew 11:1).

# 5

## Bible Prescribed Parenting Pathway before the Child's Twelfth Birthday

What follows in this chapter is a list of twelve terms that start with the letter 'A'. Parents can evaluate their parenting choices and determine how closely they match the parenting concepts of Mary and Joseph as described in the Bible according to these twelve terms. Parents adopt their own parenting styles. Families uphold specific standards of child rearing. Communities set diverse child safeguard principles. Nations follow child protection policies. The Bible prescribes Mary and Joseph's way of parenting, which anyone can choose to follow.

# (1.) Annually

## What do you and your child regularly do together? Working together with your child could strengthen your parent-child relationship.

'*His parents went to Jerusalem every year at the Feast of the Passover*' (Luke 2:41).

The celebration of the festival occurs yearly. This is a reflection of how compulsory in nature, customary in attendance, and important in observance this was to the family. The festival and the act of its celebration ultimately and so easily became part and parcel of their child's nature. Mary and Joseph showed their child the lifestyle to adopt.

In today's world, governments, through a structural educational system, work hard and put a lot of effort into supporting children academically. In the same way, parents should refuse to sit back and watch, but in cooperation with teachers, they should fulfil their parental responsibility by taking part in their child's academic and additional training needs. The aim of schooling is to give the child the best education and ensure that he or she gains appropriate knowledge and acquires rightful future skills. The training should not be shifted and left to the teachers only; instead, parents also need to instil good family values in their children and prepare them for the life ahead. In the long run, parents must rely on their insight and realize that equipping their children for the future goes beyond schooling alone and merges into the consideration of the totality of the child as a human being.

At the child's twelfth birthday or just before then, most parents would comment of their own child as an angel and would normally name this child best among others. Likewise, most children see their parents as heroes, and it is common to find them confidently commending their parents as best among others. These two parties attain a mutual equivalence of parent to child trust. This is the point in their relationship where both the parent and the child can only find the best in each other. At this level, the perspective of both the parent and the child allows them to be highly receptive to each other, and the relationship is sincere and at its best. This moment of mutual relationship may only last for a limited period, may be rare in occurrence, and may be given to chance; and thus it should not be wasted or taken for granted. Instead, all parents should grab and take advantage of every available opportunity and dedicate themselves to teaching, instructing, and guiding their children. This is the best time for parents to start preparing their children mentally and psychologically as they catch up with and align themselves to the world system while endeavouring to remain within the required morals. This is when the world and friends' influences gradually unfold and slowly shift the child's attention from the usual home confinement.

In most education systems, children move from primary to secondary schools at eleven or twelve years of age. Elementary education, also known as primary school, is compulsory and important and each child has a right to this education. Here, children receive the foundation that forms the basis of advancement, entails the acquisition of basic knowledge and skills, and determines future learning abilities. Therefore, it is best to teach the values that parents want for their children at this foundation level. It is much easier to teach a child who is below the age of twelve than it is to teach older children.

Most children over this age start to demonstrate independence and participate in their own private life affairs; thus they are inclined to question outside opinions, including those from their own parents. This should not be classified as rudeness or as argumentative behaviour, as some parents commonly do. Parents should explain and clarify their ideas and opinions, rather than impose them on the child. Only then will there be a reduction in the child's resistance. A child who is given the chance to fulfil his or her teeming potential normally attains the set goals and achieves greatly. A child who is restricted from attaining his or her full potential will stagnate or be put off in life. Parents need to grant their child freedom in order to win his or her cooperation and participation.

However, finding balance in terms of how much freedom is required becomes the most challenging part on the parents' side. For example, a child who would like to spend time with his or her friends needs freedom. But just how much freedom he or she has should be discussed and agreed on by both child and parent. Limits should be set in all things so as to avoid extremes and sustain a healthy balance.

A child whose level of understanding remains stagnate despite outward physical growth poses a concern, and the parents of such a child need to take extra care. Every child is a great achiever at his or her level best, and this fact should not be ignored. For example, a dyslexic child is an achiever at his or her own level best. This child's only desire is that his or her parents do things like give extra input in his or her work; spend more time with him or her; and seek advice, support, and help from the appropriate resources. Similarly, when it comes to nurturing, caring parents worry if their growing child does not show the expected degree of maturity or advancement.

Mary and Joseph instilled the right family values in their child; and before He turned twelve, their child evidenced progression. The mutual rapport that had been established between these parents and their child meant that they never experienced any difficulty in trying to convince their child to follow after the customary family practices and values. It is obvious that well before the child's momentous age of twelve, they had already made the feast of the Passover a compulsory family celebration. This is an indication of a parenting technique that shows how children greatly benefit from their upbringing and their parents' way of living. This adoptable upbringing demonstrated by these two parents gives significance to the idea that charity is supposed to begin at home, but now especially before the child's twelfth birthday.

We should pass on the values and practices that we wish to uphold as basic and compulsory within our families at the child's earliest age. After the age of twelve, the child enters the venturesome teenage phase, which has its own coping difficulties—mainly due to the hormonal changes that take place during this phase. As opportunities arise, holding discussions that enlighten and give your child more knowledge means the child will be prepared to face life's wider issues. It is good to be available as your child tackles and solves matters that affect him or her, but more importantly, you should adapt an open communication system that lets the child take charge him or herself. This is one way of saying that you are still walking with the child despite his or her age. A listening ear, as opposed to talking and questioning, allows for a pressure-free environment in which the child is willing and able to disclose more information. In maintaining openness, respect, and honesty on each end, every parental effort transcends into support, encouragement, and prayers for the child. Most importantly, parents must do things together with their children.

## (2.) *Accordingly*

### By what principles do you bring up your child? These principles could define your parental values and beliefs.

*'And when He was twelve years old, they went up to Jerusalem according to the custom of the feast'* (Luke 2:42).

Jesus obeyed His parents, followed their instructions, and went with them to Jerusalem. He emulated and adapted to His parents' routines by taking an action that later manifested as His vision and goal. At the age of twelve, He acted on what He would teach about in future. In childhood, He lived by the example of what He would institute in His adulthood; for actions speak louder than words. This gave more power to the words that have impacted the present world when He spoke of little children: *'But when Jesus saw it, He was greatly displeased and said to them, "Let the little children to come to Me, and do not forbid them; for of such is the kingdom of God"'* (Mark 10:14). Jesus' habit of going to God's house started with His parents; but as He grew up, He also adopted the practice, became sure of its benefits, defended it, spoke of it, and passed it on. He was ready to see to it that this practice He learnt from His early years continued into the future.

Mary and Joseph are an example of parents who valued the practice of taking their child to God's house, and when the boy grew up, He held onto that value. It is good that His parents took Him to the temple, for they are counted as the useful vessels that set off the beginning of their son's habit of loving God's house. Before the boy turned twelve, His parents played the major role of getting Him established into the practice that they themselves loved. This was the very place that He was meant to be, the place where He belonged and will forever abide; *'they brought Him to Jerusalem, to present Him to the Lord'* (Luke 2:22b).

Our children may carry visions or ideas that need developing and bringing into reality. Thus, parents should watch, examine, and pay attention to their child's way of living, preferences, choices, and abilities. Every keen parent can see, hear, perceive, distinguish, and pick up intentions from the child's daily routines. The deeds of a child and the utterances that come out of his or her mouth need parental attention, understanding, and consideration. The actions and the words of a child always display the ideas, feelings, values, and insights he or she possesses inside.

Any parent who has a child under the age of seven can bear me witness that, at this age, the child almost talks and acts non-stop. In most cases, if you keenly watch and understand this child, his or her verbal utterances and physical expressions will line up. This is a child who will sing, talk, and act at the same time. These children will fearlessly role model an adult through talking, singing, and acting. This child brings to the surface his or her inner thoughts through his or her actions and speech. This is a child, for example, who plays the teacher game and, at the same time, counts the numbers that he or she has learned in school by playing the pupil game. Children can hardly keep anything inside them before speaking or acting it out. Parents should watch and listen because these very deeds and words could be a reflection of what will shape your child's future. Missing out on these deeds and words that come from your child is comparable to a lost opportunity. A child who continually role-plays teaching could possess some teaching skills. A child who is always role-playing or talking about doctors and nurses could end up in a hospital career. A child who is always playing with building blocks could end up in a constructive career. These childhood actions and statements can be meaningfully connected together and cultivated into adulthood.

One wonders why the disciples decided to rebuke and deny parents the opportunity of bringing their little children to Jesus. In response to this decision, parents may have shied away and denied their little children the special and blessed touch of Jesus. The introduction of new rules and regulations and changes in the society could have been the contributing factors to the disciples' resolution. This decision could also have arisen from within themselves. On the other hand, it could have been the tactic of the enemy, the devil, who threatens and instils fear in those who want to follow after the commandments of God. '*Be sober, be vigilant; because your adversary the devil walks about like a roaring lion, seeking whom he may devour*' (1 Peter 5:8).

However, before the obstacles were founded, our victorious master and Lord Jesus so easily overpowered and overcame them by displaying the practice beforehand. At the word of His command and by the displeasure of His comment, everything was settled; and this stopped all the intentions, the forces, and the obstructing activities that were intended for working against this practice. He perceived danger, and took an immediate corrective action to combat this. '*But when Jesus saw it, He was greatly displeased and said to them, "Let the little children come to Me, and do not forbid them; for of such is the kingdom of God"*' (Mark 10: 14).

This same Jesus is alive today, and parents' simple duty is to take their children to Him. The transformation that comes from Him impacts humanity eternally for the good. Men would search through all eternity and never find a man on earth with outstanding living compared to His. He alone stands unchallenged, and we should take care not to miss out on His life-transforming touch. Inasmuch as parents have the freedom of choice, our children are not exempted from the touch of Jesus and its impact.

The difference that counts in life is the ability of an individual to rightly target and reach for the best, longest lasting, and most beneficial options in life. The act of taking children to Jesus was only a simulate to what the disciples already knew; and thus their attempt to forbid parents from doing so meant choosing to oppose the societal and religious practices that they all had been exposed to. The disciples' step could have resulted in denying parents permission to offer that which was good for their children, blocking children's access to Jesus and acting against the will of Jesus. Presumably for the disciples, this practice of taking children to Jesus matched their own childhood experience of having been taken to God's house during their childhood, and thus they were required to stand up for and speak up for this custom. Their decision could have arisen from personal choices, outside world influences, or surrounding inconveniences and misunderstandings; but whatever the case, they opted to forbid the children, just as many present parents still do. We must clearly note that the disciples' attempt to bar the children did not render the custom of bringing children to God powerless or unprofitable; instead it reinforced the benefits of doing so.

Jesus' immediate and thorough rebuke clearly reveals that the disciples' action fell far from the will of God. His vision was to propagate the practice far and wide into the future and through all generations. Unlike His disciples and those who were around Him, only Jesus held onto this vision and positively visualized it into the present. He alone clearly visualizes our children's future, and we should not let the words that come from human beings restrict or stop us from giving our children what so rightfully belongs to them. When it comes to expounding on the love of Jesus for children, the following verse is commonly read : '*But when Jesus saw it, He was greatly displeased and said to them, "Let the little children come to Me, and do not forbid them; for of such is the kingdom of God"* (Mark 10:14).

The moment Jesus spoke these powerful words, He established the importance of allowing children to know Him and enabling them to establish a growing and lasting relationship with Him. When Jesus was a baby, He was also presented to the Lord by His parents: '*Now when the days of her purification according to the law of Moses were completed, they brought Him to Jerusalem to present Him to the Lord*' (Luke 2:22). Perhaps the fact that Jesus' parents had been obedient to God's commandments in His childhood influenced Him when He acted to preserve the tradition of parents bringing their children to Him. He is the real defender of this practice, which His parents exemplified as part of their family custom. Any willing parent can follow after this practice and gain from its evidenced end results—the successful life of Jesus. This is the upbringing that Jesus benefited from, and His parents achieved for Him the blessing, '*for of such is the kingdom of God*' (Mark 10:14b). This upbringing can be emulated, inherited, copied, picked up, learned, grasped, stood for, upheld, and by all and for all.

# (3.) *Absence*

**At what point does your child sneak and
do things behind your back?
Being prepared for the possibility that this might
happen refines your parental care and concern.**

*'When they had finished the days, as they returned, the Boy
Jesus lingered behind in Jerusalem. And Joseph and His
mother did not know it'* (Luke 2:43).

The above scripture gives an impression and a picture
of a child who initially follows after his or her parent's
instructions, but later, something different triggers this
normal behaviour. When Jesus was twelve years old, His
parents went to Jerusalem with Him to celebrate the Passover
feast. Without His parents' permission, He stayed behind
after the celebration. Mary and Joseph were unaware of
their child's whereabouts, and they determined to go back
and look for Him.

When they found Him, they did not understand His
question: *'Why did you seek Me? Did you not know that I
must be about My Father's business?'* (Luke 2:49). It is
impossible to exactly know your child's plans and thoughts.
However, it is important to understand that most children
who are older than twelve want to take to their own
stands and embrace their own decision-making initiative.
There is no explanation given as to why Jesus decided to
stay behind without consulting His parents. However we
know that Jesus was at the age when children undergo
sudden transformations, and experience the desire for
independence. He must have skilfully scanned and planned
for an opportunity that would allow Him to tarry behind

without His parents noticing. Mary and Joseph were probably strict and overprotective, just as most parents tend to be. Just as no parent would dare want their child exposed to harsh challenges, these parents were liable to find it hard to leave their young child behind, especially amongst the learned teachers of the law. Therefore, the chances that they would grant Him permission to stay behind were slim. If He was to make such a request, it would likely be declined. He must have assumed that if He asked, His parents would deny His request. Thus, just as any other child would have, He decided to hide His plans from His parents. The lesson here is that, as a child approaches the age of twelve, it becomes necessary for parents to loosen some of the strings they may have so tightly tied around their child. Any child at this age desires freedom, trust, and permission. Alteration of some parental regulations becomes necessary in order to accommodate the child's decisions.

Parents need to respect their child's choices. They need to allow the child to positively develop his or her decision-making ability by noticing and nurturing the child's capabilities and cautiously permitting his or her explorations. The sneaking habit is bound to occur and recur in children, but parents can avoid this by exercising flexibility through reasoning together with their children and agreeing with them to adjust to one another's opinions. It is important to build a bond of trust through assurance, encouragement, and cultivation of openness on both ends. When this trust is finally obtained, its maintenance forms the basis required for the achievement of a healthy and a mutual child-parent relationship.

# *(4.)* *Assumption*

**What assumptions do you have about your child?**
**Being aware of your preconceived notions about your**
**child could expose your parental ties.**

*'But supposing Him to have been in the company, they went*
*a day's journey, and sought Him among their relatives and*
*acquaintances'* (Luke 2:44).

It is likely that the social world had suddenly dawned on Jesus. On approaching the age of twelve, most children tend to increasingly and unexpectedly gain interest in social engagements. This may hit the family by surprise, just as it happened in the case of Mary and Joseph. Nowadays, a child may show this awareness of the social world by starting to engage in social gatherings like parties and online chats; displaying increased interest in the Internet, phone texts, and calls; making new friends; and developing a tendency to stay away from home. The world of friends and the habit of staying away from the usual home environment becomes more fascinating and appealing to the child. The time spent with old or new friends starts to increase, whilst the time spent at home with parents and siblings gradually decreases. Rather than nagging the child to stay at home, parents can attach value to the little time that the child does spend at home. As children grow old, the quantity of time parents spend together with them tends to lessen. Parents ought to take into consideration how to utilize the remaining time with their children and increase the quality of that time.

If one contemplates what happened when Jesus turned twelve, we find that, for the first time He stayed behind; spoke in public; and stunningly, directly, and surprisingly posed a question to His parents. His parents must have come to a realization that they needed to adapt to a different way of handling Him. The initial step they took—remaining quiet—was presumably the best and wisest thing to do at that time. This was their form of maintaining an atmosphere that fostered two-way communication with their son. The situation probably demanded listening ears, rather than a mouth with quick answers and questions. They exercised a virtue of quietness that is found lacking in most parents. If parents refuse to refrain from the habit of quick questioning and answering back, then disagreements, anger, and quarrels will unnecessarily arise. If the ratio of spoken words to heard words is not maintained at one to two, then people have failed to understand why human beings have one mouth and two ears. '*So then, my beloved brethren, let every man be swift to hear, slow to speak, slow to wrath*' (James 1:19).

It is not recorded that Mary and Joseph became angered at the action and the words of their child; rather their quietness is noted. We read in Proverbs, '*A quick tempered man acts foolishly . . .*' (Proverbs 14:17). This is a form of patience that most present parents lack. It is only natural that most parents answer back more quickly than required, question more than needed, and demand clarification of the events on the spot. In the case of these two parents, we learn that they did not question further or seek clarification in public; rather, they waited for a private moment to arise. Some issues are best addressed on arriving home—in the closet, behind the scenes, and after calming down. Whatever the case, watching our words before speaking and waiting for the appropriate time to speak is a better way of handling any matter. '*A soft answer turns away wrath, but a harsh word stirs up anger*' (Proverbs 15:1).

Maintaining a tranquil environment by way of presenting a calm attitude and waiting for our anger to settle down before speaking ensures that we achieve a better picture of both parties' views. In any communication chain, this, in return, ensures good reception and appropriate response from both ends. '*A word fitly spoken is like apples of gold in settings of silver*' (Proverbs 25:11). Mary and Joseph were godly parents, and their child followed their Godly upbringing. Their child was neither found among His kinsfolk nor his acquaintances, but He kept a company that was acceptable to His parents. When they could not find Him among His kinsfolk or among His acquaintances, they went back to the temple to look for Him and found Him safe. They were right in thinking that the next place He would be was the temple. This suggests that the company or associates He fancied outside of His family was that of temple dwellers or goers.

The child's interest of going to the temple was initiated by His parents. Jesus picked up this habit and unconditionally kept it to the extent of defending it. '*But when Jesus saw it, He was greatly displeased and said to them, "Let the little children come to Me, and do not forbid them; for of such is the kingdom of God"*' (Mark 10:14).

It was not a wonder for these parents to search for their child within the temple, for this is where He was found. This was the place with the right company and with people who shared the same interests as His family. A place that fascinated these parents later became the very place that captured their child's first and lasting interest. Their search for Jesus began in the most probable places, just as most searches for lost items begin in the usual places among those who were in first contact with them. In the case of a lost coin, instinct leads us to search in a visibly torn pocket or flip through an obviously broken safe. The temple was definitely the most obvious and safest place to find Jesus. This was the family's treasured place. *'For where your treasure is, there your heart will be also'* (Luke 12:34). This was the rightful place to begin the search before extending it outside. This was the place with proceedings and agendas suitable to the whole family. The happenings and the people within this place influenced and moulded the entire family. It was, therefore, their child's rightful preference to tarry in the temple. This rightful preference came out of the whole family's conviction. The true message regarding the effect of parenting on childhood is conveyed by solid family convictions.

It is unfortunate that most parents underestimate the fact that they are meant to be role models to their children. Parents influence children in many ways and should take care when it comes to the places they go, the words they speak, and the company they keep, as well as the aspirations they pursue and the values they uphold. The environment that our children get exposed to matters a great deal. Children copy and eventually fall into their parents' habits. In any child's eyes, his or her parent is always right. Whatever happens in childhood shapes the child's future and sticks in his or her mind. Unless the bad examples and messages of the past get rightfully erased or replaced, the child is liable to experience no change in habit. The example that parents set is important; the choices parents make model for the child what he or she will prioritize. When we come to God, our children are drawn towards Him. When we resist God, our children do likewise.

The transition from childhood into adulthood brings the grown-up child into a position of accountability for his own decisions. Once a child has reached adulthood, any disobedience or disconnection from parental instructions should not be connected to parental failure. However, we must realize that adulthood is mostly shaped by what happens in childhood. It thus becomes complicated for people to think that they can avoid taking responsibility for the end results of their parental input. This is because the experiences of childhood affect adulthood and the two phases interconnect in such a way that what happens in childhood contributes positively or negatively to the child's future life. It should be remembered that this does not occur in the opposite way, and thus, if parents fail to instruct their children or if they deny their children that which rightfully belongs to them, then they must realize that parental failure or ignorance is part of the real problem. I will use an example of a child who asks for permission to attend a friend's birthday party. The child's parents may decide to decline the request or they may decide to allow their child to attend this party but with particular agreed upon parental instructions. These instructions could include the time the child goes to the party, the time he or she returns, whether or not the parent should accompany the child, and behaviour limitations. The parents in this case should first discuss with their child the nature of the party plans, the hours of the day that the party is being held, and other such details. Inasmuch as your child needs the opportunity to be with his or her peer group, you should prioritize the child's right to be protected from bad influences, insecure places and times, behaviours that violate the child's and the family's beliefs or dignity, and other such circumstances. The sole reason for all these choices is to come to a common ground whilst giving preference to the child's wellbeing.

It is easier to shape a child than it is to shape an adult, and childhood experiences can be damaging and irreversible. Unless one has the intentions of breaking the already hardened adulthood, it would still be hard to shape an adult. This can be compared to how easy it is to fell a small tree before it grows into a big one and to fell a large tree before it dries up and hardens. A dried-up tree splits into irregular pieces during the process of being cut, and thus one must apply special techniques and facilities when chopping it. It is, thus, less complicated to chop a small tree the way it is easier to deal with children than adults. People give a lot of significance and attention to the warranties that are attached to new machines. It is sad that such warranties only last for a limited period of time, and as the machines get old, owners need to think about conditional renewal of insurances. At no time should children be compared to machines, but the life of a child should be valued more than the machines that people seem to attach more value to.

Every newborn baby and growing child deserves the best input from his or her Maker. It is hard to tell at what point and for what reasons most parents decide to withdraw their newborn babies or young children from the care of their Maker, who is the giver of life and the best protector and supporter. The choice of withdrawing or breaking from the right of a warranty or insurance is open to the holder. A warranty needs to be confirmed through application and observed for an expiry period; insurance needs to be obeyed through policies and maintained through premiums. You must, without ignorance, observe the terms and conditions that bind you in both these cases. Those instructions that appear in small script and below the main manuscript are the ones that apply most and matter when it comes to your claim. It is important for the warranty or policy holder to pay special attention to every bit of writing, large or small, that appears within the agreement. A person's understanding of the tiny script on a contract acts as proof of his or her understanding of what he or she has committed self to. Most people immediately confirm their warranties and purchase insurance policies due to keenness to save money. Repairs to and replacements of machinery and parts is expensive. Attached to the warranties and insurance policies are terms, conditions, and policies that demand compliance. In most cases, people understand and strictly follow these terms, conditions, and policies for the sake of redeeming their items or properties. The example of warranties and insurances cannot be compared to the value of a child but the functioning method of these warranties and insurances can be applied in child rearing. *'All scripture is given to by inspiration of God, and is profitable for doctrine, for reproof, for correction, for instruction in righteousness'* (2 Timothy 3:16). The warranties and the insurances we come in agreement with have their terms and conditions, and the Bible has got more for us, but: *'Whom will he teach knowledge? And whom will he make to understand the message? Those just weaned from milk? Those just drawn from the breasts? For precept must be upon precept, precept upon precept, Line upon line, line upon line, Here a little, there a little'* (Isaiah 28:9-10). Children have been given to us by God and put in our household for a reason. They not only deserve the life insurances that they may have to take in future, but they need to be placed in the hand of their Maker.

In all our pursuits, it is important to watch out, lest we miss out on the important marks in life through ignorance. *'My people are destroyed for lack of knowledge. Because you have rejected knowledge, I also will reject you from being priest for me; because you have forgotten the law of your God, I also will forget your children'* (Hosea 4:6). If one does not know what is required of him or her in the terms and conditions of an insurance policy, then he or she will not adhere to the required steps or precautions and will be penalized or terminated from the coverage. Insurance coverage will lapse as soon as we fail to keep up with our premiums. If we receive warning, then we need to take heed and act accordingly. In the same way, parents are, most of the time, forewarned, but they fail to act according to the knowledge provided. An example of this is where parents fail to seek help when faced with issues of life that they and their child are incapable of handling.

If we take the habits with which people generally protect their machinery as an illustration of the value they attach to that machinery, we can see a definite warning—we are paying more attention on things that are short-lived than on our children's long lives. Making valuable investments in the child's childhood is a treasure, and the end results are more rewarding than the value attached to machinery. The Word of God is part of what we should be investing in our children. '*All scripture is given by inspiration of God, and is profitable for doctrine, for reproof, for correction, for instruction in righteousness*' (2 Timothy 3:16). In this scripture, we find that God has provided all that is needed to teach, reproof, correct, and instruct our children. If we remain ignorant about this, then it becomes true that we will perish for lack of knowledge. '*Therefore my people have gone into captivity, because they have no knowledge; their honourable men are famished, and their multitude dried up with thirst*' (Isaiah 5:13).

The Word of God is available for our taking and for application to life's situations, but if we do not utilize it, then we end up with dryness, thirst, and hunger, and perishing becomes inevitable. That which is eternal is there for our grabbing before it is taken away by the enemy of humanity. '*And from the days of John the Baptist until now the kingdom of heaven suffers violence, and the violent take it by force'* (Matthew 11:12). Childhood can only be lived once in a lifetime, and then after that, adulthood follows faster than anyone would think. Childhood can only last for a set period of time, and that is why this period should be well utilized. Parents should certainly give their children the best things today and not tomorrow, when childhood will be no more. A child should be given the best of experiences that he or she can benefit from, even to the point of violent passion for the plan; *'the kingdom of heaven suffers violence and the violent take it by force'* (Matthew 11:12b). The violence that is spoken of comes into play because, in most cases, it seems easy for parents to work extra shifts or overtime for the sake of providing for the physical needs of their child, but it becomes very hard to spend one hour in a week for the sake of taking the child to God's house.

It is only by doing this that we can follow in the footsteps of the parents of Jesus and in His own example. It is easy to get hold of the things of this world because our human senses can identify with them, but the things of the Kingdom of God cannot be felt by our physical bodies, and this could explain the struggle, disbelief, and doubt that follow before we receive our portion.

Mary and Joseph put effort in when it comes to bringing up their child. If this was not important, then they shouldn't have bothered taking their child to the house of God; after all, good things had already been spoken about their child. Taking their child to the house of God is one of the efforts they put in as parents. Likewise, it is required of us as parents that we put effort into getting what we can and giving it to our growing children. If, as parents, we can work hard by daily going to work so that we can save up for our children, then in the same way we can at least sacrifice one day in a week to take our children to the house of God. We should not forget that it is the spiritual things that the adversary of our souls would make it hard for us to reach for, and that is why we are advised, *'Be sober, be vigilant; because your adversary the devil walks about like a roaring lion, seeking whom he may devour'* (1 Peter 5:8).

If things that come our way seem hard to get hold of, then we have to grab or take them by violence. There is no room for taking chances, just as there is only one period for childhood in a person's lifetime. Life is what everyone has today, and tomorrow is in God's hands. As long as the 'today' time of your child exists, the best thing to do is to give the child what you consider best for him or her. Thus, the child should enjoy and be happy during the childhood that only exists today; tomorrow he or she will be in adulthood, with its own troubles. If today is rightly sorted out, then tomorrow is fixed as well.

The core point here is that, inasmuch as it is easy to give your child all that you can get hold of in this world, you should take care not to miss out on the spiritual things that are vital and yet not outwardly obvious. *'The secret things belong to the Lord our God, but those things which are revealed belong to us and to our children forever, that we may do all the words of this law'* (Deuteronomy 29:29). Take care of your child today and not to tomorrow, when he or she may enter adulthood. Take care of today, and tomorrow will have its own worries. *'Therefore do not worry about tomorrow, for tomorrow will worry about its own things. Sufficient for today is its own trouble"* (Matthew 6:34). A positive outlook during childhood easily results in an optimistic adulthood. Beyond the phases of childhood and adulthood, lies an eternity that we can see only if we focus beyond today's barriers. Mary and Joseph found it necessary to bring up their child in a way that did not shun the eternity of God's Kingdom. This kingdom demands earnestness from its partakers because it faces forceful oppositions and attacks.

The requirement that the law of God be a part of the childhood of Jesus sets a typical example of the start and the end of what childhood entails. It is not a wonder then that His life faced danger at birth. '*Now when they had departed, behold, an angel of the Lord appeared to Joseph in a dream, saying, "Arise, take the young Child and His mother, flee to Egypt, and stay there until I bring you word; for Herod will seek the young Child to destroy Him*' (Mathew 2:13). This can also be seen in a different angle, whereby we find that Jesus was not exempted from fierce, threatening, and opposing forces of life. If destruction is to be avoided and eternity embraced, then it is good to hide our children in the safety of their Maker. Mary and Joseph were keen to listen to what God had to say about their child, even in regards to the child's physical safety. In the same way parents need to follow after God's instructions and obey Him. Mary and Joseph thrived in their parenting because they obeyed God and followed after God's instructions. '*Now when Herod was dead, behold, an angel of the Lord appeared in a dream to Joseph in Egypt, saying, "Arise, take the young Child and His mother, and go to the land of Israel, for those who sought the young Child's life are dead*"' (Mathew 2:19).

Parental failure to combat the opposing forces of life endangers the child's physical, mental, and spiritual life. Foundational nurturing is required for the solid and progressive growth of the child's soul, spirit, and body. Neglecting any of these parts affects the whole being and can only be compared to an attempt to rip a portion from its only preferred residence. Developing defence strategies like determination and increased interest towards the word of God; and intense passion and enthusiasm form the valiant strategies that aid us in achieving what the Kingdom of God can offer. Although the violent things that violently oppose our children's progress should be handled violently, striking and maintaining a balance in the experiences that come from the surrounding world and from the Kingdom of God is what gives life a positive impact and meaning. The child's Maker has already paid the price.

Parenting without adherence to God's instructions is like operating a machine without the expected guidelines. This places the child at risk, but God's full assurance stands unchallenged when we come to know of it. '*For God so loved the World that He gave His only begotten Son, that whoever believes in Him should not perish but have eternal life*' (John 3:16). Both the *believing* and the *receiving* are important aspects that remind us that God does not hold a contract with us. Whatever is needed for our lives and the life of our children has already been achieved through the *life*, the *death*, and the *Resurrection* of the Son of God. This full assurance surpasses the world's warranties and insurance policies, which are regulated by terms, conditions, and policies that are subject to change, twist, and lapse. Most manufacturers are kind and sensible enough to offer an extension of warranties by offering insurance policies, but as for God and His son, you are meant to be more than sure. As it is written of Him, '*"I am the Alpha and the Omega, the Beginning and the End," says the Lord, "who is and was and is to come, the Almighty."* (Revelation 1:8). The full assurance of God extends beyond our children to our children's children and to generations that follow.

Although personal choices often apply, we can only expect our children to copy us because our actions speak louder than our words. Children are prone to imitate parents, and the child's conscience is likely to record his or her actions as failure if he or she fails to do so. This is probably the rightful and the pleasing thing for children to do. The boundaries that parents set aid in keeping their children safe. If by any chance a child crosses these boundaries, a reminder to the child normally leads to the required correction.

There are, of course, cases in which the child acts in a way that is beyond what the parent can handle. A parent in this state needs to seek appropriate help, support, and counsel. Help and support are always available for both child and parent. We should not forget that God can bring such a child back. '*The Lord is merciful and gracious, slow to anger, and abounding in mercy*' (Psalms 103:8).

At the age of twelve, Jesus asked His parents a question that suggested that He was meant to be in the right place at the right time. As any responsible parent would, His parents panicked when He went missing. At that particular time and age, it was possible for these parents not to have yet understood the predestined plan for their child's life. It is, however, an encouragement that God's plans for every child's life cannot be thwarted. He knows our children better than we do. It is in personalizing and linking the Word of God to our children that we understand what He says about our children. '*Before I formed you in the womb I knew you; before you were born I sanctified you; I ordained you a prophet to the nations*' (Jeremiah 1:5). God has got greater plans for our children, and He is the master planner of every child's life. '*For I know the thoughts that I think toward you, says the Lord, thoughts of peace and not evil, to give you a future and a hope*' (Jeremiah 29:11). God understands your child better than you do, He knows your child's ways better than you do, and He has the best thoughts about your child. He is more conversant with your child than you are. *'How precious also are Your thoughts to me, O God! How great is the sum of them! If I should count them, they would be more in number than the sand; when I awake, I am still with You'* (Psalms 139:17-18). It is important for parents to release their children into God's able hands. This will save them the anxiety of parenting. Jesus is the forerunner of childhood, and His parents are the forerunners of ideal parenting. It is essential that we hold onto God's promises and place our children into His caring and able hands, *'casting all your care upon Him, for He cares for you'* (1 Peter 5:7).

## (5.) *Accountability*

**What do you give up for the sake of your child?
What you give up for your child's sake could reveal
your parental commitments.**

*'So when they did not find Him, they returned to Jerusalem, seeking Him'* (Luke 2: 45).

As children approach the age of twelve, they tend to become more explorative. This is the stage where some parents start to think that their child is drifting away or experimenting with things he or she is too young for. If parents grasp the fact that Jesus started by first experimenting with the things that His parents had exposed Him to, then the pains, the fears, and the anxieties that come along at this phase are unwarranted. The temple was the place where Jesus' parents always took Him. The teaching of the law was the main activity that took place in the temple. This place was the first place Mary and Joseph looked when they searched for young Jesus. Mary and Joseph's prior actions showed their approval of this place, along with the people and the activities within it. It can, therefore, be concluded that Jesus was in the right place, with the right company, and doing the right thing. This confirms that it is important for parents to be careful when it comes to the places they go, the things they do, and the company they keep when they are with their children. The lifestyle that adults adopt testifies to the children and impacts them more than we may think. It is best for parents to avoid the things in the present that they will disapprove in the future. If we were to examine a child's future lifestyle and we were to detect priorities and disciplines that fall in line with those that the parents displayed in the presence of that child, we should not be surprised.

Jesus first spoke in public when He was twelve years old. There is a big gap in the recording of events that might have taken place before Jesus reached adulthood and entered into His ministry. He seems to have disappeared from the scene after He first spoke in public. The fact that He took to teaching when He next appeared in adulthood proves that He carried His childhood dream of teaching purposefully forward. The old treasured childhood habit was carried into adulthood, and He eventually came up as a qualified teacher. This can be compared to the way our children take time to go away for studies and later come back qualified and having gained experience and skills. At the age of twelve, a child needs a lot of support and encouragement in order to start and stay with the routines of regular studies. Like any present-day parent of a twelve-year-old child, Mary and Joseph must have been faced with the challenge and the battle of helping their child stay focused and concentrate to the end. It is natural that, when a child gets credit, the parents get credit too. When the child works hard and attains qualification, parents are also believed to have worked hard. Both the child and the parent eventually share the end results of success. This explains why both parents and children equally share in the pride and the joy of every graduation ceremony, along with their family at large.

Although in its discussion of the upbringing of Jesus, the Bible doesn't talk about His studies, Mary and Joseph must have endeavoured to do their best in aiding their child as He expressed His full potential. Whatever Jesus expressed in His childhood is what He became in adulthood. This suggests that His parents nurtured and prepared Him well for the future He aspired for since childhood. He is the greatest teacher. He survived the teen years and successfully passed into adulthood.

A child's future does not entirely rely on his or her parents' efforts, but parental contributions are necessary in shaping the child's preferences. Jesus' following of God's predestined plan for His life should make us realize that the plans that God has for our children are great and beyond the human limit. Jesus grew up, lived, and related to people naturally. He learned, acquired, and used the human language to carry out His teachings. He conveyed all His messages at the human level of understanding. The efficiency of His mission prevailed in a natural presentation of messages and teachings. If He would have decided, instead, to do it supernaturally, neither His parents nor anyone else would have understood and reached Him. The end results of His performance would not have been as productive and exceedingly immeasurable as at the present.

In ages past through the present, Jesus' teaching remain extremely productive, immeasurable, and incomparable, and they guarantee a lasting remembrance. The world has ever and will forever embrace His teaching and Him as a teacher.

Mary and Joseph went back to look for their child, and on being found, the child followed them back home. Their going back and the child's acceptance to follow them are two vital steps that hold a big lesson. We can liken their going back to the occasional need to review and find out what has been lost in our parenting flavour. Going back is a healthy step, and the greatest part of this is the ability to accept the child back after a mess. It is not uncommon for children to walk out on their parents, but during these moments, it is the parents' responsibility to go out and search for the child, just as Mary and Joseph did. These two parents went searching; they did not wait for reverse to happen. On finding the child or on discovering the child's deviations from the family norms, at no time should parents build barriers that would hinder them from accepting or welcoming the child back home.

The responsibility of winning back the lost relationship should not be shifted and left to the already seemingly lost child. This will only burden the child with unbearable pain, and he or she will think of finding other ways to escape. The child may not understand the other dangers that lie in the way, and he or she is prone to become more lost. This explains why the alarm of concern rang in Mary and Joseph in that, although their child had always been on this route to Jerusalem, they did not decide to leave it up to Him to make His way back home. These parents must have been prompted to act swiftly by the uncertainty of where their child was, the unpredictable length of time He would take before coming back, and the fear for His safety.

Ideal parenting should not be burdensome, but parents should be triggered to show acceptance, accountability, attention, affirmation, and affection to their children. Although children rely on their parents for correction, they should also be made to accept accountability for their own actions. Children need to be listened to; we must pay attention to them and understand that their views are vital. Children need support from their parents; constant reassurance builds their confidence. Children need to be loved, and the affirmation that this love is unconditional allays all their fears and doubts. Children should be loved affectionately, but acceptance and restoration should be part of the relationship.

In the case of Mary and Joseph, they always availed themselves and created time to take their child to the temple. They provided emotional support by physically accompanying their child to and from the temple. They took care of their child's social well-being by taking Him to gatherings alongside His acquaintances, whom He easily socialized and associated with. They provided a chance for Him to sit among the learned teachers of the law; He thus gained intellectual knowledge. They took their child to the temple; this provided Him the chance to hear the Word of God. They lived their practical life in a Godly way, and their child grew spiritually. The trips to Jerusalem and the vicinities thereof were recreational and refreshing, comparable to the yearly family holidays that people save up for.

The child's route of growth and developmental may seem unfamiliar, but Mary and Joseph are an example of parents who familiarized themselves with their child's behavioural changes. '*Even a child is known by his deeds, whether what he does is pure and right*' (Proverbs 20:11). At each stage of their child's life, Mary and Joseph built confidence in Him and identified the potentials He possessed. At one time, Jesus was not ready to do something extra, was not willing to attempt something new, and did not seem to realize that His time had matured, but His mother, who was conversant with His growth and development, pointed this out to Him. *'And when they ran out of wine, the mother of Jesus said to Him, "They have no wine." Jesus said to her, "Woman, what does your concern have to do with me? My hour has not yet come." His mother said to the servants, "Whatever He says to you, do it."* (John 2: 3-5).

There was a wedding in Cana and the wine ran out of stock during the celebration. Mary the mother of Jesus pointed out this shortage to Jesus. She wanted Him to deal with the situation; she trusted that He was able to do it. This was an emergent situation, and it needed someone who could act fast or handle it. Jesus was the only one who could deal with this, and that is why Mary called on Him this time. This was a wedding, and a great supply of wine was required. Mary was sure that Jesus was capable of meeting this demand. Mary was sure that this was the appropriate time and that Jesus was the right person to bring the solution. If not, then she would not have asked Him; she would not have asked her son to step into a situation far beyond what He could handle. She was not a mother who would want to embarrass her child in the event that things did not work out. It is only natural that, in case of any emergency, we tend to run to the person who we are confident can meet our need. Mary knew that Jesus was able and ready to do this, and yet He could have been sitting among His mates in the comfort zone.

This is a lesson to all parents when it comes to setting targets and goals for the child; these goals should be achievable, realistic, and relevant to the child's interest. Mary reported this matter to Jesus and not to anyone else, and this reflects the total confidence that she had in her son's ability.

Even though Jesus questioned her—'*Woman, what does your concern have to do with me?*' (John 2:4a) she knew that He was capable of doing it. It was her personal concern, and she did not have to involve Jesus. Even though He declared what seems to have been His deeper heartfelt feeling—'*My hour has not yet come*' (John 2:4b)—Mary knew that He was capable of doing it. As if the above statements from her Son were not enough to make her think otherwise, she still stressed the point by saying, '*Whatever He says to you, do it* (John 2: 5). This was in public place, just as was the temple where Jesus was found speaking when He was twelve years of age. Mary must have visualized her son's ability, and she was perfectly sure that Jesus would do it. He stood out in the temple when He was twelve years old, and Mary knew that He would stand out wisely again.

I am sure that Mary could have thought of other means of replenishing the wine, or she could have simply declared the shortage, but she still bothered to call her son. Why did she get concerned to the point of involving her son? Like anyone else, she could have just as well kept quiet and let things go their own way. She mightn't have bothered herself, but she chose to be bothered and to the point of disturbing her son. Jesus could also have chosen to sit back like anyone else and pretend like nothing was amiss. His mother pointed out the need to Him; as many parents do, she called her child aside to assign an extra task that the child was capable of doing. She insisted, as if speaking out for a child who does not seem to have a voice, especially due to some form of obstruction. In our lives, when an emergency arises, we are normally quick to identify the person who can quickly deal with the situation at hand and without any hesitation. This is what Mary saw in Jesus—someone to call upon in the event of a crisis. Jesus gave a reply that indicates some reluctance towards the challenge He faced. But as for Mary, His mother, this was the right time, and she was clearly right, as we can see. Mary had heard so much of her child from the time of conception, and by then, she knew that Jesus was divine. Jesus' ability to perform miracles was not limited, and neither Mary herself nor anyone else at the wedding could have managed to limit Him. She thus did not believe that any limitations to perform miracles existed in her child. She must have felt desperate about the situation, to the point of believing that this was the right time and the right place for this miracle.

Jesus was human, like us. In the human sense, we find that He was about to limit Himself from doing something that He was capable of doing, just as most of parents and a great number of our children do. It is good that His mother was able to pinpoint His potential and call Him out of the crowd. As is sometimes the case with our children, He seemed to be in the hiding place when He should have been at service. If our children do not use their full potential, then they miss out on opportunities, they waste their efforts and time, and they delay their privileges. Parents need to stand by their children and be forefront in encouraging or supporting them as they step forwards and achieve life goals. There is no need for parents to keep quiet when their children are allowing what they come across to limit them. Although it is hard to read a child's particular phase of life, we should avoid limiting capable children. '*Counsel in the heart of man is like deep water, but a man of understanding will draw it out*' (Proverbs 20:5). Mary made her child realize the hidden gift in Him.

It should, however, be remembered that, inasmuch as it is good to step forwards and help your child realize his or her potential, it is far better to step back and let the child do everything at his or her competence level. We read that Mary pointed out the need to her son, but when it came to what should be done, she stepped back and said that the servants should do what He said. In the same manner, parents should only aid their child and should not get involved in what he or she is doing. This is the same as guiding your child through his or her homework as opposed to literally doing it for the child. Only in the former case will the child understand what he or she is doing and master the subject at hand or stay on top of his or her studies.

Mary and Joseph sacrificed their time, postponed their businesses, and made a one-day trip back to Jerusalem in search of their lost child. Going back searching for Him cost them time and energy. They spent the majority of their journey walking, as, for the most part, other means of transport weren't available. Unlike in ancient days, diverse methods of transportation and communication make it much easier to keep in touch nowadays. Improved communication technology, including cell phones and social networking, has brought the cost and the convenience of keeping in touch within favourable and advantageous limits. This, in turn, eliminates all common excuses of leaving children on their own and unguided. Not all children at the age of twelve may understand the importance of keeping close or in touch with their parents. Where possible, children should be reminded, counselled, cautioned, and encouraged on the importance of keeping close or in touch with their parents. A bond of trust built on both ends forms the basis of freedom in any relationship. Although moments of conflicting issues commonly occur and cause both parties of a relationship to worry, we can quell any arising dissatisfactions by accepting each other's mistakes and coming to an agreement. The big problems that may arise can be solved by keeping a balance between acceptance and agreement. Anyone who harbours things on the inside only destroys bridges, making it difficult or impossible to cross over to the other side, but voicing, disclosing, and bringing out our thoughts through discussions builds bridges and creates a clear and navigable pathway for progress. It has been said that 'children know no malice,' and as such, parents will always remain the determining factor when it comes to honestly expressing concealed feelings and achieving the desired result.

When making inquiries, parents should not be given to the habit of doubting what their children tell them. Suppose Mary and Joseph had doubted their child; they would only have created a feeling of mistrust in their child, whom they found in the temple just as they thought they would. We learn from this that, at times, when we should be thanking God for what is unfolding in our children, we tend to dwell on feelings of doubt and disappointment for too long, and thus, the real track of our child's development gets missed out. Adopt the habit of checking on your child as part of parenting. Checking on the child is not bad at all, but you should follow certain limitations and ensure that you are motivated to check only out of the care and the love you have for the child. If you overuse this privilege, your child will likely build resistance and, thus, start keeping secrets tightly; and he or she is bound to see your behaviour as irritating or embarrassing.

There are many ways a parent can keep in touch with the child, including offering necessary physical company, giving needed help, providing required escort, sending a text message if distance has to be kept, picking up the child where possible, and being available to cheer up the child. Parents should avoid disappointments by keeping their promises. They should inform the child of any changes early enough. Children quite often get disappointed and lose trust if parents don't keep their promises. If circumstances change and you are not, for example, able to pick up your child, then it is better to inform your child ahead of time or seek to arrange alternative means of transportation.

Children's cooperation is needed when it comes to what parents can do for them. In most cases, if the child has grown up in the habit of keeping in touch with the parent, then this will continue as he or she grows older. However, regardless of the obstacles they encounter, the doubts they face, the problems they experience, and the sorts of reports they receive, parents should not give up on their children. As long as your child is alive, there is still hope and room for change.

## (6.) *Acceptance*

### What would you accept from your child?
### What you accept from your child could challenge
### your parental priorities.

*'Now so it was that after three days they found Him in the temple, sitting in the midst of the teachers, both listening to them and asking them questions'* (Luke 2:46).

By sitting down to listen to the Word of God, Jesus clearly demonstrated to us that we and our children should also sit down and listen to God. Inasmuch as it is good for our children to sit among, listen to, and seek answers from professionals, it is also recommendable that they sit at the feet of those who proclaim the Word of God. One day, Jesus spoke of words that clarified the urgent priorities of two sisters that He visited: '*And Jesus answered and said to her, "Martha, Martha, you are worried and troubled about many things. But one thing is needed, and Mary has chosen that good part, which will not be taken away from her"* (Luke 10: 41-42). Considering the good and the bad habits that we have learned and developed, we should take seriously the mandate that we need to sit down to listen to God's word, as demonstrated by Jesus. In the above verse, both Martha and Mary were out to do their best in their areas of talents. I can imagine Martha coming up with the best meal for the day. I can also imagine Mary paying all the attention needed for good learning. But, Mary's act was recommended! We learn from this that that we should spare time for God. I am sure, unless otherwise, Jesus must have informed this family in advance that He was going to pay them a visit. The two sisters ought to have prepared ahead of time or set their priorities aright so that the sole purpose of Jesus' visit could be accomplished. Martha simulates those individuals who arrange nice conferences and yet get engaged in other activities at the time when the speaker is addressing the assembly. The sole purpose of such a conference becomes futile. Ignoring God's word as a family denies us and our children the opportunity to pay attention to it; and it is risky. During the proclamation of the Word of God, individuals get physical, spiritual and psychological healing. The many areas that need healing in our families and communities get missed out due to deviated attention to the Word of God.

We and our children can only have faith through the Word of God. '*So then faith comes by hearing, and hearing by the word of God*' (Romans 10:17). In God's presence, there is power that can work in us and in our children, allowing us to reach things in our lives that may be hidden. '*Now it happened on a certain day, as He was teaching, that there were Pharisees and teachers of the law sitting by, who had come out of every town of Galilee, Judea, and Jerusalem. And the power of the Lord was present to heal them'* (Luke 5:17). The very food needed for living can only be found in Jesus, the Son of God. *'Do not labor for the food which perishes, but for the food which endures to everlasting life, which the son of Man will give you, because God the Father has set His seal on Him'* (John 6: 27). All human beings are made for their creator, *'for in Him we live and move and have our being, as also some of your own poets have said, For we are also His offering'* (Acts 17:28). To find God is to find everything we need to live. *'But seek first the kingdom of God and His righteousness, and all these things shall be added to you'* (Matthew 6: 33).

It is common to find a twelve-year-old child exploring and experimenting with the things that he or she has learned in the past. It's not a surprise to find your child trying on things like watching television programs meant for an older audience, downloading and playing games on the Internet, and spending a lot of time communicating online with friends. The 'curiosity that killed the cat' is the primary reason for most of this exploration, and it only poses danger if parents don't guide the child through the process.

Most parents are astonished and disappointed upon discovering that their child has indulged in habits they disapprove of. A child may become involved in harsh experiences, and he or she may make mistakes. For example, children may extensively explore dangerous places, enter into partnerships with bad company, take in bad or unsafe reading materials, or gain access to insecure Internet sites and downloads. In the big picture of life, they are likely to drop all of these habits. These harsh experiences and mistakes can thus be corrected, and reasonable change can be achieved. Most parents, at times, do paint their own version of the big picture, wherein shallow shadows seem deep. We can avoid overindulging in negative thinking by explaining to our children what they are allowed and not allowed to do. Children do finally reach an agreement and take to better and good decisions.

Just as is common with any twelve-year-old child, Jesus decided to explore. He explored the law of God and the temple's conduct and contacts. We can only speculate about His parents' reaction to this situation. Certainly, they would have felt relief at finding their child. They must have experienced the climax of this relief in the peace that their burdened hearts received on finding out that their child was in the place they expected; He was among the preferred people and doing what they themselves treasured in life. It is certainly natural that they felt no regrets about this. Mary and Joseph must have embraced and appreciated the fact that their child was starting to fall in line with their interests and approvals. Parents always feel rewarded when they see their children engaging with the world in a way that meets their approvals. Parents can, henceforth, start a more focused nurturing process that aims to bring the child's talents, gifts or abilities to full maturity. Jesus did and said a number of things for the first time. He chose to stay at the temple. He dared stay behind from His parents. He sat alone among the teachers of the law. He spoke in public. He clarified the course and the purpose of His life. He declared God as His father. The diligence of His questions and answers amazed the hearers and set Him apart.

It is most probable that such words of wisdom were not expected to come from the mouth of a twelve-year-old child. This makes Jesus the forerunner of every child. No matter the outlook of things, every child is a carrier of an unfolding vision, hope, and future, and all care needs to be observed so that the child's potential is not unknowingly limited. Your child may show artistic talent, but because you are a teacher, you may be tempted to think that your child should pursue a teaching career like yours. If Joseph had one mentality and thought that Jesus would end up in carpentry just like him, then he would have been disappointed to discover that the interests of Jesus did not fall in line with his own as a parent.

It was good to see Jesus firmly standing up for what He knew was true inside Him. When His parents sought Him, He said to them, '*Why did you seek Me? Did you not know that I must be about My Father's business?*' (Luke 2:49). The carpentry family business was not what Jesus could manage. The manner by which we handle our child's interests and strengths determines the growth of his or her dreams and hopes. This is also largely dependent upon how early we start encouraging our child's talent from the very point of discovery, since the child's vision will always be there but his or her dreams and hopes might be carelessly patterned. In return, the home atmosphere will always positively or negatively count towards the child's future.

On finding out that their child has attempted a daring thing, most parents will promptly, unwisely, and without thought take inappropriate corrective actions. We can avoid these unforeseen pitfalls by taking time to keenly listen to the still whisper that comes from God and paying attention to what the child is saying. As a caring father, Joseph would have wished that his child take up a carpentry career, but this was not the case. The religious lifestyle of these parents deserved emulation, and this is what captured their child's whole being. The child Jesus, who grew up naturally, followed the course of His vision of teaching into the future, and His parents did not impose this career on Him. The teachers of the law were respectable members of the society, and yet Jesus, as a child, was found among them—not only just sitting and listening but also talking. This daring step that Jesus took might have been named 'courage' by the encouragers, or it might have been counted as 'disrespect' by the discouragers. We will always find both encouragers and discouragers in our societies, but parents should advocate for their children when things go differently from what was expected.

Jesus' parents handled and viewed this differently from how most present parents would; the outcome of which did not affect or kill their child's vision. The way the disciples stopped children from meeting Jesus seems to evidence that children were not allowed to get forefront and meet or intermingle with religious leaders or people of prestige. When Mary and Joseph discovered that Jesus had decided to not only sit among the teachers of the law but also to ask them questions, they did not harshly rebuke Him and deter His dream, but instead, they seem to have lavished good parental support upon His dream, helping Him stay focused and working together as a family towards one common goal. He greatly succeeded in His first area of aspiration and emerged as a great teacher in adulthood. '*Now Jesus Himself began His ministry at about thirty years of age, being (as was supposed) the son of Joseph . . .*' (Luke 3:23). The accomplishment of childhood dreams normally evidences and gives a scenario of full parental support.

As He grew and developed, Jesus underwent what our children go through when they withdraw from their normal routines, families, and environments to pursue studies. '*Then Jesus returned in the power of the Spirit to Galilee, and news of Him went out through all surrounding region. And*

*He taught in their synagogues, being glorified by all'* (Luke 4:14-15).Travelling or taking time away from home allows children to allot ample time towards concentrating on their professional development. In His adulthood, Jesus confidently, efficiently, and boldly resurfaced into His ministry. *'So He came to Nazareth, where He had been brought up. And as His custom was, He went into the synagogue on the Sabbath day, and stood up to read'* (Luke 4:16).

Just as older children step into careers, younger children may step into challenging situations and new responsibilities, like preparing for exams. Parents need to stay beside such children for the purpose of building their confidence and aiding them in facing the world positively, boldly, and purposefully. However, God is besides your child with a strength that is greater than you could ever imagine. *'Now to Him who is able to do exceedingly abundantly and above all that we ask or think, according to the power that works in us, to Him be glory in the Church by Christ Jesus to all generations, forever and ever. Amen'* (Ephesians 3:20 - 21). God is on our side and on the side of our children. *'What then shall we say to these things? If God is for us, who can be against us? He who did not spare His own Son, but delivered Him for us all, how shall He not with him also freely give us all things?'* (Romans 8:31-32).

The best products that are manufactured normally come out of the original ingredients as opposed to counterfeit ingredients. This applies to letting your child know the Word of God and know Jesus. Jesus is the very Word of God. The Word of God can shape your child better than other information around him or her. *'And the Word became flesh and dwelt among us, and we beheld His glory, the glory as of the only begotten of the Father, full of grace and truth'* (John 1:14). Jesus knew that God's word and the God's chosen will were inseparable and necessary things to abide with. In His childhood, He sat down to listen to God's word, and this was the right thing to do. In adulthood, He encouraged the habit of sitting down to listen to God's word, and this is the best decision we can make. You can trust Jesus to help your child, since He is the very one who God gave to us. We can found the treasure of God's Word in our children by allowing them to be among the teachers, the hearers, and the searchers of God's Word.

## (7.) *Ability*

**What abilities have you discovered in your child? The discovery of these abilities could unleash the hidden treasures in your child.**

'And all who heard Him were astonished at His understanding and answers' (Luke 2:47).

Jesus' self-assertiveness and focus distinctively came into appearance in such a way that no one could stop His purpose. Neither the world's opinions nor opposition prevailed against Him. He was predestined to reach His destination.

Present-day education systems and parents spend a great deal of funds towards imparting skills such as self-assertiveness and good goal setting practices to their children. In most institutions, this aim has given root to programs designed to give guidance and advice and to the incorporation of mentoring and assertiveness courses within educational institutions. The whole aim is to bring into existence what the child needs to possess in order to achieve in life.

God's wisdom surpasses the world's wisdom, and that is why Jesus as a child had a level of understanding that has prevailed in the record of remembrance. '*The fear of the Lord is the beginning of wisdom, and the knowledge of the Holy One is understanding*' (Proverbs 9:10). Jesus knew His Father, the Holy One, and His praise would forever endure. '*And Jesus increased in wisdom and stature, and in favor with God and men*' (Luke 2:52). We can, therefore, attain the very wisdom that is needed for success in life by knowing Jesus. '*But we preach Christ crucified, to the Jews a stumbling block and to the Greeks foolishness, but to those who are called, both Jews and Greeks, Christ the power of God and the wisdom of God*' (1 Corinthians 1: 23-24). Jesus grew in favour with God and people; likewise, every child is destined to receive this favour. Jesus had reached the age of twelve. The number *twelve* is an important number in the Bible. Consider the following examples:

1. *Twelve*—the age at which Jesus first spoke in public (Luke 2:42, 46-47)
2. *Twelve* disciples *(Matthew 10:1)*
3. *Twelve* sons of Jacob (Exodus 28: 21)
4. *Twelve* gates of the New Jerusalem (Revelation 21:12)
5. *Twelve* fruits of the tree of life (Revelation 22:2)
6. *Twelve* tribes of Israel (Genesis 49:28)
7. *Twelve* angels at the gates of the New Jerusalem (Revelation 21:12)
8. *Twelve* foundation stones (Revelation 21: 14)

This might be an eye opener to parents in terms of the significance of their child's twelfth year. On parents' part, the main appeal is to lay a foundation that the child is able to build on. This foundation is best laid before the child turns *twelve* and with the child's Maker involved through His Word. In the child's upbringing, it is basically best to place the Maker in the centre of family life. Only then can we as parents make it easier for our children to find a reference point that will help them to make any necessary life repairs. The original manual should always be available and the first place we run when we diagnose a fault or a problem with our mechanical machines. The Word of God is the reference point from the child's Maker.

We can observe the importance of the age of twelve in the world's education systems. In today's education systems, a child typically moves to a higher level of education on or around his or her twelfth birthday. Whatever the case, the move from primary to secondary life is never far from your child's twelfth birthday. In most cases, at this preteen age, the child moves from year *six* to year *seven* of his or her formal education. The number *six* in the child's education can be related to the *sixth* day in the story of creation. The child's sixth year in formal education is the time of completing primary school as well. The number *seven* in your child' education can be related to the seventh day in the story of creation, when God completed His work and rested. '*Then God saw everything that He had made, and indeed it was very good. So the evening and the morning were the sixth day. Thus the heavens and the earth, and all the host of them, were finished. And on the seventh day God ended His work which He had done, and He rested on the seventh day from all His work which He had done*' (Genesis 1:31 and 2:1-2). It is only normal for people to sit or lie down to rest upon completion of a task or a project that they have been engaged in. Along the child's educational path, before he or she steps from primary into secondary school, he or she should experience a sense of completeness deserving of a period that provides rest.

There number *seven* is also an important number in the Bible and appears several times in the scriptures as seen below:

1. God ended His work on the *seventh* day. He rested on the *seventh* day (Genesis 2:2).
2. God blessed the *seventh* day and sanctified it (Genesis 2:3).
3. Noah took with him *seven* each of every clean animal (Genesis 7: 2).
4. Noah took *seven* each of the birds of the air (Genesis 7:3).
5. God caused it to rain on the earth after *seven* more days (Genesis 7: 4).
6. *Seven* honest men were set before the apostles (Acts 6: 5-6).
7. The fire furnace was heated *seven* times more than usual (Daniel 3:19).
8. *Seven* priests bore *seven* trumpets (Joshua 6:4).
9. The wall of Jericho collapsed on the *seventh* day (Joshua 6:15).
10. *Seven* stars, *seven* churches, and *seven* lamp stands are mentioned (Revelation 1:20).

This is only a partial list of the places where the Bible mentions the number *seven*. The significance of the number *seven* demonstrates that the child's seventh level of education is important. The main aim in addressing this topic on figures is to enlighten parents and the government on the importance of laying the child's growth and developmental foundation before the year seven of education (secondary education) and before the preteen age.

The future of every nation is laid upon today's children. We must maintain equilibrium between the governmental contributions and parental inputs towards our children's growth and development requirements. We must maintain equilibrium within the physical, the psychological, and the spiritual needs of the child. Since the achievement of this balance seems to target a particular age group and timeframe in the world's education systems, then children's accomplishments are bound to be unique if this interlinking juncture is achieved. At the age of twelve, children are most likely to impact the world like Jesus did. At the age of twelve, children display unique potentials that could be harnessed for the benefit of families, neighbourhoods, communities, and nations at large. Those who heard Jesus speak at the age of twelve experienced astonishment and could not comprehend His words within their human minds. This simply illustrates that children need Jesus' example in their lives before they reach the age of twelve. This preteen age lies between the developmental phase (the years before the child's twelfth birthday) and the self-realization stage (the age of twelve onwards) when the child starts to demonstrate the inner power he or she possesses. At the age of twelve, children strongly display the desire to be able to accomplish things on their own; the phrase, 'I want to do it my own way' characterizes this stage well. Jesus conquered this phase of life wisely. When faced by the authorities, He did not keep quiet regarding His Father's Word. When asked by His parents the reason for tarrying behind, He made it clear that He must be about His Father's business.

Maintaining a healthy balance between the child's ability to make his or her own solid decisions and the parent's ability to accept and handle these decisions requires wisdom. The self-realization stage seems to suddenly surface up in most children, just as it happened in the case of Jesus. The fact that everyone was amazed at His words and His mother Mary had no words to say implies that this new found sign of maturity occurred as a surprise, when no one was prepared to handle it.

However, there is much we can learn by examining the way that Mary and Joseph handled the situation. It is important to manage any conflicts that may arise at this point well; the failure to do so will result in the beginning of a strained child-parent relationship. If the strained relationship spreads into or beyond your child's teenage years, then it will become more hard for such a child to handle conflicts in future. We can reverse this negative effect on the child's future by teaching the child how to rightly resolve the conflicts that arise in childhood. This conflict resolution skill is best instilled in the child at the earliest possible age. Developing a good filtration system when it comes to your opinions will ensure that you do not completely disregard your child's ideas, discouraging and making your child kick back. If this happens, then the child will, instead, habitually withdraw or resist.

Since practice is the best teacher, an individual's practices tend to teach others more about the person than anything else. The child as an observer eventually forms his or her life's routines from the practices that he or she so easily copies from his or her parents. This is because your practices are displayed in actions that speak louder than your words. Parents need to always explain the reasons behind the boundaries they set, the beliefs they uphold, and the practices they engage in. The good and the bad experiences that the child undergoes are not meant to destroy but to correct and construct him or her.

If parents lose good relationship with their children, this relationship should normally be restored, just as in the case of the prodigal son. This is a story in the Bible about a father and his two sons. The younger son demanded his share of the family wealth. The man divided his livelihood and gave the younger son his portion of the division. The young son gathered all that belonged to him and travelled to a far country. There, he wasted his possessions with extravagant living. When this wasteful son had spent all that he had, he began to be in want. The only way out of this situation was to go back to his father and ask to be hired as a servant. *'And he arose and came to his father. But when he was still a great way off, his father saw him and had compassion, and ran and fell on his neck and kissed him'* (Luke 15:20). The parental role should be to guide, protect, and love your child. In the case that your child makes bad decisions and strays away from the family norms, you should always *welcome* your child back whenever that child comes to his or her senses.

# (8.) *Affinity*

## What anxieties do you have for your child? Managing your anxieties rightly could lighten your parental burdens.

*'So when they saw Him, they were amazed; and His mother said unto Him, "Son, why have You done this to us? Look, Your father and I have sought You anxiously"'* (Luke 2: 48).

Out of parental concern, most parents despair and worry about their children, instead of being thankful to God. Surprisingly, some parents think that withholding their child from God is a way of showing love and protection. And yet other parents act in a way similar to this by practicing give-and-take behaviour, handing their child to God and yet refusing to let go. As parents, we need to realize that we cannot love our children more than God does. The safest place for our children to be is in God's able hand. *'Behold, the Lord GOD shall come with a strong hand, and His arm shall rule for Him; behold, His reward is with Him, and His work is before Him'* (Isaiah 40:10). Only by releasing their children to God will parents experience true inner peace in parenting and unleash their children's full potential. It is only God's *perfect will* that can set both parents and children at *liberty*.

We are admonished, *'Be anxious for nothing, but in everything by prayer and supplication, with thanksgiving, let your requests be made known to God; and the peace of God, which surpasses all understanding, will guard your hearts and minds through Christ Jesus'* (Philippians 4:6-7). Jesus had already discovered the rightful place of abiding, and yet His parents still worried. Their prayer of committing the child to

God had already been answered, and yet they did not realize this. Jesus was already in God's control, and yet they still sought to exercise parental control. Their child was peaceful and resting in God's able hands, and yet they themselves remained restless and disturbed. Their child was already feasting at the serving of God's Word, and yet they struggled within. Their heart's desire regarding the child's future had already been fulfilled, and yet they still desired differently. The child was meant to be at God's business, and yet to them, He was meant to be with them or among His kinsmen. They had always taken the child to the temple and let Him listen to God's teachings from the law. When it came to the child's future, they must have desired that their child be at the temple, and surely they must have desired that He sit down to listen to God's law. '*So then faith comes by hearing, and hearing by the word of God*' (Romans 10: 17).

In our lives, we take children to schools, clubs, day care centres, gyms, and many other places for the sake of them benefiting from the services available in our communities, gaining knowledge, and fitting into the available routines. Mary and Joseph's case is no exception, and their child had no choice but to copy and live by what He had been exposed to. When we doubt, fear, and worry, then we have not given God full control over our lives and the lives of our children. By exercising faith in prayer, we hand our children over to God.

At this stage in Jesus' life—when He turned twelve— Mary and Joseph could not have monitored His whereabouts nor held Him back; only God could give the best care here. This applies to every parent and the children that God has given us. '*Commit your way to the LORD, trust also in Him. And He shall bring it to pass*' (Psalms 37:5). Characteristically, when we have reached our very end, God exercises His will and power in the situations of our lives. If you do let God take complete charge of your child's life, then the elements of sorrow, anxiety, and questioning will cease from your life. The Word of God is able to penetrate into the inner parts of the child's life that parents cannot reach. '*For the word of God is living and powerful, and sharper than any two-edged sword, piercing even to the division of soul and spirit, and of joints and marrow, and is a discerner of the thoughts and intents of the heart*' (Hebrew 4:12). The Word of God is God Himself. '*In the beginning was the Word, and the Word was with God, and the Word was God*' (John 1:1). This means that it is possible for your child to be even safer than you can comprehend.

## (9.) *Agenda*

**What plans have you set for your child?**
**Knowing these plans could be the fulfilment of your parental program.**

'*And He said to them, "Why did you seek Me? Did you not know that I must be about My Father's business?*' (Luke 2:49).

Governments, through the world education system, have it right in that, by the time children turn twelve, the level of education is valued and extended by graduating students from elementary school to high school. The level of knowledge that is progressively instilled in students is normally measured by educators in terms of age appropriateness. The students will have already acquired the foundational knowledge necessary for them to learn and incorporate the new information they receive. At each level of education there are challenges to face, but these students eventually manage to prevail in their education. If the age of *twelve* is of significance to governments, then it is only right that we invest as much as we can in these children by making them realize how much they are valued in the society. This in turn will strengthen the child's abilities that meet the future governmental goals.

The age of twelve marks the stepping stone into the teenage years. There may be a lot of stumbling blocks to climb over, but with God, all things are possible. If all parents purposefully focus their efforts within the family, ensuring that their target is to build up what they have discovered in their child before his or her twelfth birthday, then the child gets the chance to tap into his or her vital potentials. The benefits and the end results at this point will be great, and the profits will extend from the individual families to the community and governments at large. If we seek to harness the skills and the potentials in our children, then the resources required for productive, responsible, and promising future citizens will not be wasted. The parents of tomorrow are the children of today. The children that we see today are the hope of future communities. The progression of each family, community, government, and the whole world relies on the fulfilment of these children's potentials. The importance of childhood is reliant on the parents acknowledging that every child has been born with a plan, a future, and a hope. The message is clear: 'Every Child Matters.' 'The aim is for every child, whatever their background or circumstances, to have the support they need to: *be healthy, stay safe, enjoy and achieve, make a positive contribution, and achieve economic well-being*' (The Children Act 2004; (Every-Child Matters).

The childhood of Jesus illustrates the best patterned master plan to emulate. We can find the future hope for which humanity seeks in the example of His lifestyle. In both His childhood and adulthood, He prevailed in the way He lived; and thus He will forever be remembered. Neither should we forget His parents, who have shown us the best way forwards in achieving our parenting goals. If it was possible for these parents to succeed, then present parents can also achieve their goals. Jesus has demonstrated that He possesses the victory and provides whatever is needed to overcome the struggles—to get past the entanglements, the stagnations, the hindrances, and the discomforts of life. These are things that would hold back our children from climbing over and reaching their potentials, but, '*Now thanks be to God who always leads us in triumph in Christ, and through us diffuses the fragrance of His Knowledge in every place*' (2 Corinthians 2:14). Jesus overcame the barriers of childhood and the teenage years, and our children can too. He challenged and defeated the wisdom that the world's system poses. He chose to learn from the learned. He acquired knowledge from the Word of God and according to God's standards. The perfection in Him unfolded and grew into full maturity, and He imparted the wisdom required to rightly handle the world and spiritual affairs to the human race.

As we have discussed, a twelve-year-old child will either be in year six or year seven of his or her schooling. The numbers *twelve* and *seven* are two important numbers in the Bible. The number *six* at this level could represent the opposing force that would want to drag your child back, displacing and preventing him or her from entering into the significant number *seven*. God's work of creation took place in *six* days, and then He rested on the *seventh* day.

This seventh day of the week has been blessed, and that is why, without question, we normally observe the custom of working for six days and resting on the seventh day. During the six days of the week, we utilize our energy in order to accomplish what we want. On the seventh day of the week, we rest from our works and the labours of our hands. If your child does not recognize the importance of putting effort into projects during the first six days of the week, then the week goes wasted. If the foundation of a child's education is not well laid by year six (at the end of primary school) and before year seven (at the start of secondary education), then this child will inevitably struggle in high school. This could lead to stagnation; it could prevent the child from achieving his or her desired destination and meeting his or her full potential.

The number *seven*, on the other hand, could stand for the driving force that wants to see your child prevail over all kinds of hindrances and step up into adulthood. This is similar to the stepping block that leads your child from childhood into his or her teenage years. The teenage phase comes with challenges that the child needs to face wisely. In comparison to primary education, secondary school education comes with higher multi-phased standards and dimensions, which children need to understand and confront. They will have different teachers for each subject and be introduced to more subjects, classes will cover topics more widely, the style of learning changes, the approach of teaching differs, and the syllabi will be different. Although the aim is to build on what the child already knows, strengthening the weak areas and polishing up what he or she has already acquired, parents need to give guidance and help so that the child will be able to cope with these enormous changes.

At this age, children's knowledge greatly increases and their ability to absorb information grows. Children need assistance developing their ability to make choices in order to tackle the challenges that come with these changes. They need to learn that they don't need to store and act on all the information they discover. They may not understand why it is even necessary to try and block some information from entering their mind. A child may not understand why filtering the information that we absorb is necessary. The child may not understand that only necessary information is important. Only when a child reaches this understanding will he or she be able to choose what is necessary and drop what is not beneficial; for example, he or she will be better at choosing which places to go to and which ones to avoid, as well as which friends to keep and which ones to drop. Help and guidance can be offered from home, schools, clubs, seminars, churches, advice and information centres, and other such resources.

We should remember that, along with good parents, school teachers, and well-wishers, there are other eager teachers in the world who wish to teach your child anything and at any cost. At the age of twelve, children are developing an inner yearning for freedom that makes them think that a concerned parent is being overprotective. Most parents tend to think of this as resistance; rather than that the growing adult in the child now trying to surface. A child at this stage seems to be participating in a higher level of self-discovery than before. This is when you should encourage your child, participating in moulding him or her to reach the full potential required. When adulthood finally kicks in, your child, in return, will be more prepared to boldly face the world and come up victoriously.

Every individual child has a part to play in his or her journey of life; thus, letting the child try things out for him or herself is one way of respecting the child's views. It is good to reflect on your own present and past mirrors as you talk over issues with your child. It is better to discuss issues together with your child than to impose your personal ideas on him or her. Building your child's confidence is wise because the world is full of eager discouragers who could spoil your child's view of life. Offering your child the support he or she needs is best because, without support at home, your child is likely to seek sympathy from outside and land in bad situations.

Parents should further build the strengths they have already identified in their children; doing so is better than pointing out the mistakes your child makes. In most cases, parents easily point out their children's mistakes but fail to point out the good things found in them. There are many ways that we can show and verbalize our appreciations; among them are gifts, words of thanks, compliments, congratulations, kisses, hugs, praise, rewards, approvals, and more. If your child behaves well, compliment him or her. If you like what your child has done, congratulate him or her. If your children have behaved well, then praise them. If they perform well in school, reward them. They deserve hugs for treating each other kindly as siblings.

Focusing on the wrong things that a child has done makes him or her behave further badly for the sake of attracting his or her parents' attention. Parents should proactively assist their children to stay focused and attain their set goals. Parents are better off avoiding staying on either the offensive or the defensive sides. Rather, parents and children should work together. For example, if a child is not performing well at school, parents should proactively assist him or her with assignments, work together with the teachers and the child, and eliminate the habit of assigning blame. In this case, the child is more liable to incline towards parental guidance. Positive construction dwells on the child's strong areas by adding onto what the child has, encouraging the child and assisting in his or her positive development. Negativity is destructive and dwells on the child's weak areas, thus giving birth to discouragement. Failing to build on the child's strengths is like failing to fill in the missing gaps in the wall of a building; such a building will collapse. The refusal to supplement for the lacks in your child is similar to ignorance and can be classified as negligence. The child cannot receive the required support if we fail to identify his or her abilities, interests, strengths, talents, and skills.

Your child's life is like a building, and its foundation needs pillars for support and strength. In addition to the foundational pillars that you have already laid in your child's childhood, you'll need to fill in the gaps and repair any cracks that would hinder your preteen from stepping into a healthy teenage life. Your teen needs to safely endure the teen years and grow and develop into adulthood. Your child's attainment of maturity is reliant upon some vital determinants and thus, in all these dealings, parents need to be aware that a child has a fragile mind, which they must nurture; a soft heart, to which they must tend; and feeble limbs, which they must support.

Parents, guardians, and teachers spend most of the time with a child before he or she reaches the age of twelve. The amount and quality of the time a child spends with these adults can almost exclusively predict his or her future character. This does not mean that we can foretell the child's future, but we can keenly pick up vital information about children from their utterances and actions. This is because, as children grow, they tend to speak their mind, role-play their favourite characters, and speak frankly about their likes and dislikes. *'For out of the abundance of the heart, the mouth speaks'* (Matthew 12:34b). When your child seems to use an abundance of words comparable to a parrot, it is worth paying attention to what the child is communicating behind the scenes. When your child seems to act speedily like a gazelle, remember that, *'Even a child is known by his deeds, whether what he does is pure and right.'* (Proverbs 20: 11). Since actions speak louder than words, the characteristics your child silently displays should not be ignored. Making your children realize the importance of what they hold in their hands will, in return, persuade them to choose what they want in life.

# *(10.)* *Admitting*

**What do you know about your child?
Admitting your own limitations could be the start of enhancing your parental knowledge.**

*'But they did not understand the statement which He spoke to them'* (Luke 2:50).

Most parents may not understand the ways, ideas, and aspirations of their preteen children. A form of fire gets kindled inside the child that tends to make him or her neither fear nor know barriers. An ignition of emotions marks the transition from childhood to adulthood. Enlightenment is needed regarding the tremendous physical, emotional, intellectual, and growth changes that the child starts to face. The rapid physical development that signals the end of childhood and the beginning of physical maturity may be dazzling to the child. Your child may find the new hormonal chemistry of his body, which leads to emotional adjustment and changes, challenging and hard to adjust to. Your child's inner fight for identity may be displacing him or her internally, as displayed in his or her external actions. The effects of an expanding social life may not be suitable to your child. In most cases, these changes and effects are liable to leave the child in crisis, full of contradictions and mix-ups.

A preteen's know-how and eagerness greatly expand, and it is common for preteen children to be fascinated with topics surrounding puberty. Parents should capture every possible opportunity and explain things to the child, as he or she may be harbouring misconceived ideas. The aim should be to clear things up and set ground rules regarding age appropriate issues, such as what it means to have a boyfriend or girlfriend; the appropriate age to start dating; how long to stay out with friends and at parties, when to go to the movies, or going other places that may require travelling away from home; when to start wearing makeup; the appropriate way of dressing; and when to start using cell phones and registering on social networking. The list of these issues may be extensive or intensive depending on individual families, but the aim is to safeguard our tender children. Children will grow up and face more complicated issues in adulthood, and it is only wise for parents to keep their children safe from heartaches and aid smooth childhood.

Although, at the age of twelve, the child may be curious and experimental, parents should be vigorous and yet gentle in guiding and setting boundaries for their children. Do this by talking openly. For example, explain the dangers of wearing makeup at an early age, such as a bad reaction to chemicals. Tell your child how beautiful her skin is so that she can take pride in it; explain to her that she can easily spoil it with makeup. Tell her that her hair is soft and lovely and her nails are soft and nice. Explain to your child the dangers of misusing the cell phone, noting ways that his or her phone number could be accessed by strangers. Keep in mind that, at the same time, the child needs to socialize with his or her friends. Lay down restrictions on social networking, ensuring that your child doesn't utilize these networks until he or she reaches the appropriate age. Explain how his or her private and confidential information could easily be exposed when on Facebook. The future effects of your child having his or her profile exposed could be detrimental. Explain to your child the importance of concentrating on schoolwork rather than starting serious relationships. Make your child aware that crushes are not to be taken seriously and that he or she may not be mature enough to handle the demands of a relationship. If he or she attempts a serious relationship, there is a high possibility that he or she will end up dealing with broken relationships because, as preteens, children are too young to handle this. Explain to your child that there is the possibility of friendships shifting as these relationships break apart and this is not what he or she wishes for. If the child has to hang out with his or her friends, then he or she should do so in a group setting or in the presence of a responsible adult, and the child should be clear on how long he or she is going to stay out.

At the age of twelve, children start to give assertive answers. They clearly demonstrate that they are engaged in self-discovery. They become logical, abstract, and idealistic in thinking and in words. It is necessary for parents to grasp that this is the time when children most need parental understanding and support, but we must not forget that God's help is highly vital. No parent should be struggling on his or her own. Instead, parents should seek help from other available sources, such as teachers and mentors at school and counselling and advice centres in the community.

# (11.) Agreement

**What do you and your child agree on?**
**Exploring the ways in which you and your child agree could challenge your parental opinions.**

*'Then He went down with them and came to Nazareth, and was subject unto them, but His mother kept all these things in her heart'* (Luke 2:51).

It is healthy and a sign of maturity when people with differing ideas reach an agreement; work around their differences; and best of all, resolve arguments. Conflict resolution is one of the qualities that we need in the present world. Reaching an agreement with your child does not mean any disrespect to you as a parent, but in most cases, doing so will prove that you see your child as an individual who can make his or her own decisions. If children have grown up under their parents' careful instruction, they will rarely make decisions that strongly contradict their parents' guidelines. Rather, most children will endeavour to be obedient to and maintain their friendship with their parents if they have received friendly parental instructions.

Mary and Joseph were God-fearing parents. Jesus was obedient to them and went with them to the place of worship. God's commandments were read in this place of worship. He became obedient to what He heard during the reading of God's commandment: '*Honor your father and your mother, that your days may be long upon the land which the Lord your God is giving you*' (Exodus 20:12). The blessing of long life has never departed from Him; He lives forever more. At the age of twelve, He wanted to spend more and more time outside and away from His family, just like most children do. Mary was left pondering the words of Jesus. It seems like this was the first time that He was not found among His kinsmen; it was the first time that He stayed behind.

In the same way, most parents are amazed by their growing children, and more so when the child reaches the preteen stage. Our children may utter words or answer us in a way that leaves us speechless or pondering, but our ability to handle such words and actions matters greatly. Just as Jesus' mother kept all these sayings in her heart, a way of showing your child that you understand is to be silent and listen. Silence and listening are two better options than giving a ready answer and delivering a speech. It is most probable that, through silence, Mary was later able to tap more information from her child. This is a better way because most children eventually fully open up and share more things with parents when they are given a listening ear instead of a pestering mouth. It shows that working in collaboration wins the child back. Silence is a virtue that was found absolute in Mary. Inasmuch as most parents cannot conceal things regarding their children for long periods, Mary managed to do so, and for that, great honour should be accredited to her as a parent.

# (12.) *Achievement*

**What value have you attached to your child?
Remembering that your child is valuable could help
you evaluate your value system.**

*'And Jesus increased in Wisdom and stature, and in favor
with God and men'* (Luke 2:52).

This is the verse that carries the theme of this book. It
summarizes the accomplishments of Jesus' parents and what
the parents of today can do in bringing up the children of
tomorrow. Jesus was a child just like any other child. Every
child should be held to a high standard when it comes to
attaining spiritual and governmental significance, just as
Jesus was. Every child has the capacity for reaching this state
and growing in favour with God and humankind, just as
Jesus did. If Jesus was alive in the present age, I am sure
that many would have voted Him into leadership because
of His qualities. The Pharisees realized that Jesus had won
the favour of the crowd by His deeds and remarked to each
other, *'You see that you are accomplishing nothing. Look, the
world has gone after Him!'* (John 12:19b). Every child has
the qualities needed in the world today.

Jesus remains the King of Kings and the Lord of Lords
to the present. He has prevailed spiritually, and yet, he
started off as a child with earthly parents. *'And being found
in appearance as a man, He humbled Himself and became
obedient to the point of death, even the death of the cross.
Therefore God also has highly exalted Him and given Him
the name which is above every name, that at the name of Jesus
every knee should bow, of those in heaven, and of those on
earth, and of those under the earth, and that every tongue*

*should confess that Jesus Christ is Lord, to the glory of God the Father'* (Philippians 2:8-12).

As children continue to grow, they increasingly become perfect in their own way, according to their own level of understanding, and at different speeds. Jesus was wise in many aspects of His life. In terms of relationships, He gained favour with God and humankind. As to His speech, He spoke with wisdom and was heard for the first time in public at the age twelve. Regarding His responses; His answers were astonishing. In the records, He will forever be spoken of. He focused on doing His Father's will. His parents managed to capture the essence of good parenting by filling in the gaps that could have interrupted their child's transition from childhood into responsible adulthood.

It is hard to comprehend how Jesus' parents would have managed to bring up Him without God's Word. They demonstrated a parenting style that is worth emulating. This is the kind of parenting that requires a high level of understanding the child and, at the same time, incorporates upholding God's commandments. Jesus needed the Word of God in His life. Our children are *also* bound to need the Word of God. From His childhood and throughout His adulthood, Jesus loved the Word of God. Our children are *also* capable of loving the Word of God. Jesus sat down to be taught God's commandments. Our children *also* can be taught the Word of God. Jesus explored God's commandments. Our children *also* need to be given the opportunity to explore the Word of God. Jesus freely took the steps necessary to live according to God's commandments. Our children *also* need the freedom to step out, move, and live in the liberty that the Word of God gives. Mary and Joseph believed in God's Word which proved to be an efficient tool for their child's upbringing. The Word of God is *also* available to aid all parents today. Mary and Joseph took the initiative of making their child understand the value of God's commandment. Present-day parents can *also* take a stand and the initiative to teach their children the Word of God. As our children grow in the wisdom and grace of God, they *also* will attain hope, maintain focus, and be blessed so that they can bless others.

# PART II

The Fundamentals

This section includes stories in which we can engage our children, while simultaneously teaching them some life principles. At times, parents find teaching their children the importance of wise choices difficult. What we deposit in our children becomes a seed that will eventually grow and that, one day, we are sure to harvest. '*While the earth remains, seedtime and harvest, cold and heat, winter and summer, and day and night shall not cease*' (Genesis 8:22). The farmer harvests what he sows. It is unlikely for a farmer to plant a maize seed and harvest beans; it is impossible for him to plant mango seeds and harvest oranges. Every fruit comes from its own kind of seed. The stories below are part of the good values that you can deposit in your child's life with the expectation that you will get a good harvest.

# 6

## Foundations

Brought up in the 1970s in a small village called Mamboleo located in the western part of the country called Kenya, Musingi lived in a community where the types of houses residents occupied matched up with the economic status of its members. The old rocky three-bedroom house in which she lived was small indeed. Musingi and her family felt that the house had tiny, squeezed, and stuffy rooms. The children shared one bedroom, and the other room was set apart as a study room. Located near the farmyard, the house stood beautifully to be admired, its ancient strong presentation distinguishing it from the neighbouring modern houses. The house had initially belonged to Musingi's grandparents, and the key was finally handed over to her dad as the inheritor. Musingi's dad had inherited this house, and because of that, her parents were hesitant to relocate. The big grassy playground around the house and the quiet neighbourhood were the other additional advantages.

A beneficial decision arose when the family expanded. The house required an extension; there was plenty of room for improvement and expansion. But financial setbacks dragged the family behind. The cost of living was inevitably high, and winning a lottery was the only possibility of fortune. Amazingly indeed, this came to pass when the family won a lump sum of money. The joy and the achievement of the family—a fulfilled dream—dawned on them. What could stop them from embarking on a project? Before long, the money had been deposited in their account, and Musingi's parents' hands were loaded with work.

Surprisingly to the children, the appealing idea of the whole family celebrating the big victory never took place. There was no mention of a holiday, a party, or some freewill expenditure. The children's highest expectation was only a wish as opposed to their parents' big plan. Musingi's parents could not afford to squander a penny, and the idea of doing so was literally far from their thoughts. They anticipated an expensive and important project ahead.

At last, the expected inherent step was taken; the family drove to Uncle Shauri's house for consultation. Finally, after a long family talk, Uncle Shauri, who was a professional architect and a good financial advisor, came to task. Musingi kept a distance and yet keenly listened to the discussion; nothing very thrilling came up. At last she captured the conclusion of the discussion, which her parents and uncle approached very seriously; it regarded home improvement plans.

The list of items to be bought seemed inexhaustible. The workbook was full of numbers, sizes, and costs of all kinds of items—steel, metal bars, gravel, concrete blocks, cement, tiles, sand and glass, and miscellaneous other materials. To Musingi these were new vocabulary words, and she picked them up very quickly. A closer and second glance at the massive list only revealed the inevitable capital-intensive and extensive plan ahead.

The construction site became out of bounds to the children. Only the photographs that Musingi's dad occasionally took gave them an idea of the building's progress. The children remained content with everything until annoying news struck them; besides taking so long, the project had consumed all the funds at the foundation level. Its presentation did not match its value since, visually, there were only the diggings, the trenches, the mud, piled up sand and soil, the rubbish skips, the mixed concrete, and the noise from the concrete mixer. At the children's best judgment, the building's foundation was appalling, unpleasant, and annoying.

Musingi's dad had to stand up and explain things—not because it was necessary that he give an account of the expenditures but because an opportunity for teaching and empowering his children had arisen. With illustrations, drawings, and explanations, he stuffed his children full of knowledge and information. He explained to them that the foundation is the most vital part of a building and that it needs to be firm in order to provide a strong support. The costly steel bars and the wire mesh that he'd bought would ensure tensile strength and hardness. He added concrete to provide reinforcement, and despite being expensive, it was essential and preferable to use cement because of its formability and longevity. He clarified how cement has replaced the rock as the longest lasting and most easily available building material, which has always been in use in the past.

Musingi's father went on to explain how all over the world news regarding environmental disasters have never ceased. He focused on natural disasters—the destructive earthquakes, the tornados, the tsunamis, the torrential rains, and the flooding, news of which would revolve in the world news as long as the earth pivots on its axis. He enlightened them on how to combat these disasters through reinforcements and use of different building materials and styles in construction. He gave examples of the various materials used in construction, including ice, thatch, brush, plastic, wood, glass, mud, clay, and rocks.

Musingi's dad had chosen the expensive material—the cement—for his building. Most of the money that he had won in the lottery was consumed by the time the foundation had been laid. However, it dawned on Musingi and her siblings that long-lasting things are expensive. This part of the house needed a strong foundation, and building a strong foundation was costly. Their dad, moreover, made them aware that the foundations that are laid in constructing houses can still be shaken, but we can only try our best to go for the resilient things of life.

This is what the Psalmist was referring to when he asked, '*If the foundations are destroyed, what can the righteous do?*' (Psalms 11:3). It's no wonder that Jesus likened His Words to a rock. '*Whoever comes to Me, and hears my sayings and does them, I will show you whom he is like: He is like a man building a house, who dug deep and laid the foundation on the rock. And when the flood arose, the stream beat vehemently against that house, and could not shake it, for it was founded on the rock. But he who heard and did nothing is like a man who built a house on the earth without a foundation, against which the stream beat vehemently; and immediately it fell. And the ruin of that house was great*' (Luke 6:47-49).

# 7

## Budget

It was Friday afternoon, and the first lesson was mathematics! Mwanafunzi did not look forward to it. Bored, he gazed through the glass window in the classroom, hoping for anything else but not another prolonged session of solving sums. Mrs Mwalimu, the mathematics teacher, approached the classroom door sooner than Mwanafunzi realised. In order to get his mind focused, he adjusted his sitting position. He managed to absorb all the information as Mrs Mwalimu introduced the subject.

Surprisingly, to Mwanafunzi and the rest of the class, in the end, the lesson was good and interesting, and it caught their attention. Mrs Mwalimu plotted a graph on the board and set the ball rolling. Based on a simple activity, with no working out of figures, the pupils were required to interpret the graph that displayed Mr Madeni's monthly income and expenditures. The suggestions, the contributions, and the feedback that the pupils gave were valuable and constructive. An initial glance exposed that the situation was clearly critical; Mr Madeni's daily expenditures exceedingly outweighed his monthly income. Despite his increasing demands, his earnings remained stagnant.

Poor Mr Madeni; he needed to do something! His financial state was in a mess and called for urgent action. Before things crumbled, before he became indebted, and before he incurred huge overdraft charges, he needed dealing with the situation.

'Quick then, class; let's think of solutions,' Mrs Mwalimu prompted the pupils.

Hands went shooting up in the air, and all sorts of answers effortlessly flowed from the mouths of the pupils. The summary of the many brilliant responses was as follows: Mr Madeni should beg from a charity, borrow money, seek for a new job, look for a good-paying job, work more hours, learn to save up for rainy days, look for an additional job, enter a lottery, apply for benefits, and reduce his daily spending.

Mrs Mwalimu decided to have a lengthy discussion on the last suggestion—reducing the daily spending. The attentive pupils were out to impress everyone; Mr Madeni needed to prioritise his needs, channel his money rightly, know his total earnings, spend within his limits, distinguish needs from wants, look for means of making some profit that could earn him some extra funds, search the market and compare prices before shopping, shop when sales and offers were on, go for quality affordable items, make second-hand purchases instead of buying brand new items, repair than replace items, and avoid instant shopping.

'Everyone deserves a pat on the back,' said the flabbergasted Mrs Mwalimu as she slowly flipped through the final pages of the lesson plan and gathered her books in preparation to leave the classroom. She digested the lesson outcome like an individual given to meditation. A radiant smile ran across her face—a smile that conveyed satisfaction but owed the children a reward. In appreciation for the pupil's participation, she ensured that everyone in the class received a budget planner and a calculator—the two simple devices that most banks and lenders use to help clients plan their finances. These tools were cheap and simple but important aids that could signal a warning if our finances were stretched beyond their limit. These two aids would save individuals from the pitfalls of debts and embarrassment.

The teacher agreed that the children had thoroughly embarked on the topic of Mr Madeni's situation and had expounded on all the necessary strategies that would help him embrace a lasting change. Their suggestions were simple, inspiring, striking, and fabulous. They embraced a big and real change. This is what the Bible asks: '*For which of you, intending to build a tower, does not sit down first and count the cost, whether he has enough to finish it—lest, after he has laid the foundation, and is not able to finish, all who see it begin to mock him, saying, "This man began to build and was not able to finish." Or what king, going to make war against another king, does not sit down first and consider whether he is able with ten thousand to meet him who comes against him with twenty thousand? Or else, while the other is still a great way off, he sends a delegation and asks conditions of peace*' (Luke 14:28-33).

# 8

---

## Friends

Ushirika had three sisters, Wamama had four, and together the girls formed a group of nine good friends. They became good neighbours too. This was not because they followed their instincts; nor was it because there were antecedent similarities among them, but because of the choice they made—to nurture their relationships.

They cared for each other and loved each other's company. In togetherness, they prayed, sung, played, shared ideas, chatted over issues, laughed, cracked jokes, giggled, narrated stories, and engaged in thrilling activities and entertainments. Their aim was to transform their friendship into a structural relationship that would be emulated and remembered in future by other people who heard of them. They took every opportunity to serve, bring up, and nurture one another; thus, they enhanced each other's lives, self-esteem, and hobbies. Their good talks and deeds had no limits. They always maintained an environment that sustained and promoted the valuable and virtuous characteristics they found in each other. Whether long or short, the time they spent together always turned out to be of good and lasting interest, and they created memories they would always treasure. The fountain of their stories never dried up, and their motives remained apparent. In moments of disagreements, these girls quickly sought and reached resolution and reconciliation.

The friends shared with one another and ensured that each of them was able to participate in whatever was going on, and their core purpose was to foster each others' interests and meet each other's needs. They interacted with mutual care, empathizing and sympathizing appropriately. They bestowed their friendship with love and grounded it on the concerns of and welfare for all. In return, their friendship richly grew and eventually deepened. As companions who embraced each other and shared the same interests, they upheld values that moved them towards their common goals. They genuinely and openly influenced and shaped each other by sharing a sense of direction and a bond of intimacy built on trust. They gained from each other's contributions of ideas and judgements, acting as a mirror to one another and each counting herself responsible for the others.

On many occasions, these friends bid one another farewell. These inevitable parting moments did not allow their vital relationships to be seized continuity. They invested time, resources, and energy in order to keep in touch with each other. They visited each other and communicated via phone calls, emails, letters, text messages, Facebook, Twitter, and online chatting. They spent a few coins on travel fares, phone bills, post cards, greeting cards, and gifts that they exchanged with each other. In all of the considerations they made and steps they took, the friends considered and preferred a healthy, hearty, lively, and enjoyable atmosphere.

Periodically, they went on group holidays. The trips were fabulous; the rooms at the hotels magnificent, spacious, and clean; the vicinities and environments they visited splendid; the swimming pools warm and massive. Best of all was the superb company they found in each other.

The group extended and developed into a network that included more new friends. These friends linked up and became acquainted with one another. Their influences on each other led them to have better relationships within their families. These good family relations formed friendly neighbourhoods. The friendly neighbourhoods combined to form a valuable community and a strong society, which transformed into a healthy nation.

Two other states—namely, Wazee and Vijana, emerged and decided to communicate the Ushirika and Wamama way of establishing healthy relationships. It was not long before this that another country called Watoto had stepped forwards in determination to hold onto a similar idea of reinforcing healthy relationships within their community. Their neighbour country, Wajukuu, was next to fall in line with the same trend. They later realized that they were meant to be always together. They formed an organization called Wakenya. This organization had one distinct policy that defeated its opponents—the *Harambee* (an event held in East Africa to raise funds for a charitable purpose), the goal of which was to tighten collaborative engagements so that the world would become a better place for everyone to live in.

In conclusion, the world has always been a place of networking with friends. This is what has led to the evolvement and creation of friend's societies; networks that reunite people; mates, pals, buddies, and chum groups; and online social networks, such as Facebook, Twitter, and the like. Friends are for our good, not for destruction; friends are to be found, not to hide; friends are to pick up, not to drop; friends give direction, not misdirection; friends draw near and do not withdraw; friends inspire and do not tire. A friend in need is a friend indeed. '*A man who has friends must himself be friendly, but there is a friend who sticks closer than a brother*' (Proverbs 18:24).

# 9

## Forgiveness

On a trip towards one common destination, two friends had a chat.

'It's thrilling to find someone in their hiding place,' said Musamaha.

'I like the noise and the running involved,' replied Deni.

'Conflicts and arguments are never absent in this game, and my sister, Mfalme, hates it when these occur,' commented Musamaha.

The friends longed for Saturday playtime. The warm summer was approaching, and the warm gatherings of friends made the day all the more special and delightful. The play was adventurous. Hide-and-seek was the most exciting and common game and the one the group enjoyed most. The sense of victory and joy the children expressed when they came from the hiding place unspotted was true, hearty, and triumphant. Dashing out from the hiding place with a shout of victory was the most liked and distinct part of the game.

On one eventful Saturday morning, the day dawned with beams of light from the sun growing bright and beautiful. Musamaha only had his sister, Mfalme, to play with. He saw no sign of other friends or neighbours coming along to play on this particular day. On the field at the peak of the game, Musamaha thought of finding an uncommon hiding place. He wanted a spot where his sister would find it difficult if not impossible to find him.

'In order for Mfalme to give up the search, I will hide behind the thicket at the edge of the fence,' he whispered to himself as he tiptoed to his secret hiding place.

It was not a wonder when, at last, the exhausted Mfalme stood still and waited for her brother, Musamaha, to jubilantly spring out of his surprise hiding place. 'I give up the search!' she announced, waiting for her brother's shout of victory.

But to her great surprise, she heard instead a terrible scream, full of hurt and fear coming from the thicket. 'Oh help, oh help! Please help! Please help!' screamed Musamaha.

'What's the matter?' asked Mfalme, perplexed. She almost took flight, but she was constrained towards a better move.

Eventually, she made the best decision and moved towards the thicket to rescue her brother. She could have chosen the worst option—the easy alternative—and opted to run away due to fright.

*What could have happened to Musamaha?* Mfalme wondered.

She heard a cry of agony from the sobbing Musamaha. 'My leg, oh my leg, it hurts awfully!' He had stepped on an extremely sharp piece of glass!

Upon determining where, specifically, her brother's howling voice came from, Mfalme responded. She arrived at the scene, gazed at her brother, and noticed a gush of blood coming from his foot. When she spotted the gash from which the blood poured, her face turned pale, and her limbs went sweaty and panicky. She saw that her brother was in excruciating pain, and she also started crying. She realized that crying along with her brother was not going to be helpful; nor was it the best choice. Her natural instinct commanded her to do what was necessary—run for help!

The sight of her brother's blood was horrendous, and she couldn't contain it—neither in her tender heart nor in her little mind. She had to seek help. She ran off like lightning, panting and with her heart thudding. The distance seemed long, but her physical body dared not give up. After all, her brother could not do the running, and she was the only one available to do it. She responded like an emergency response team.

The image of her brother's blood was horrendous and stuck in her mind. The vision proved hard to bear and to erase, and she needed able and caring hands to offload everything into.

'Mum and Dad, must come and see this.' Mfalme whimpered as she ran. 'Musamaha's profusely bleeding!' she gasped when she found her parents.

Soon the astonished parents were at Musamaha's side. The fragment of glass embedded in Musamaha's foot had penetrated his skin deeply and could only be removed under general anaesthesia. This was the only option availed on arriving at the hospital. The family members experienced their saddest moment ever that evening as they quietly and trustingly clung to each other, waiting for Musamaha to come out of the operating theatre.

Deni and his dad headed off to the hospital to pay a visit. Deni was Musamaha's best friend; the boys were schoolmates and playmates too. Upon arriving at the extensive ward, father and son could not easily find Musamaha.

'Musamaha's best game is hide-and-seek, and I am sure he could be hiding!' remarked the anxious Deni.

Without realising, he began the search. He wandered off until he bumped into a helpful nurse, who instructed him on where to find his friend.

'I am hiding here,' Musamaha called out from the opposite room.

'No, Musamaha, I found you, and it's now my turn to do the hiding!' protested Deni.

'You did not find me. I called out for you!" Musamaha retorted firmly.

'You always do this, Musamaha!' replied Deni, almost roaring back.

He was, luckily, restrained from an emotional outburst by his dad. His dad reminded the boys that they were in hospital and not on the playground and that maintaining quietness was paramount.

'When will this ever stop? You always end up in disagreements, quarrels, and grudges,' Mfalme, who was also present at the visit, said, fiercely reprimanding the boys.

'I can tell that you are all angry,' Musamaha's dad interrupted, aiming to help the children reconcile their differences.

He narrated a Bible story that required all of them to reconsider their opinions and their similar predicaments. They finally chortled and resolved their quarrel with forgiveness. This is the best choice, as illustrated by the following parable:

*Jesus said to him, 'I do not say to you, up to seven times, but up to seventy times seven. 'Therefore the Kingdom of heaven is like a certain king who wanted to settle accounts with his servants. And when he had begun to settle accounts, one* was brought to him who owed him ten thousand talents. But he was not able to pay, his master commanded that he be sold, with his wife and children and all that he had, and that payment be made. The servant therefore fell down before him, saying, "Master, have patience with me, and I will pay you all." Then the master of that servant was moved with compassion, released him, and forgave him the debt."

'But the servant went out and found one of his fellow servants who owed him a hundred denarii; and he laid hands on him and took him by the throat, saying, "Pay me what you owe!" So his fellow servant fell down at his feet and begged him, saying, "Have patience with me, and I will pay you all." And he would not, but went and threw him into prison till he should pay the debt. So when his fellow servants saw what had been done, they were very grieved, and came and told their master all that had been done. Then his master, after he had called him, said to him, "You wicked servant! I forgave you all that debt because you begged me. Should you not also have had compassion on your fellow servant, just as I had pity on you?" And his master was angry, and delivered him to the torturers until he should pay all that was due to him. So My heavenly Father also will do to you if each of you, from his heart, does not forgive his brother his trespasses.' (Mathew 18:23-35)

# 10

## Choices

Grazing and watering the cattle at the riverbank had become the norm. The animals were always thirsty after the heat of the day. Mujukuu and his grandpa would walk down the hills as the animals grazed along the way. Any that wandered off the track would be flogged. The refreshing breeze of the evening wind blew on the faces of Mujukuu and his grandpa as they strolled on.

This particular day seemed to hold a lot for Mujukuu to learn. As soon as they reached the riverbank, his grandpa sat on the ground. He looked tired and yet calm as he breathed in the gusty cool air. Mujukuu could tell that his grandpa yearned for some silence and rest. His grandpa never seemed to take time to rest. He would always rise early before everyone else, and by the time the grandchildren were up for school, he would be out of the compound on the farm. The only times he would sit down were the treasured meagre mealtimes when he would narrate stories to his grandchildren. The day would end with all of them reading the Bible and saying a word of prayer. The grandparents would then retire to bed whilst Mujukuu and his two younger brothers would gather around the table for an hour of study and homework.

The cattle had quenched their thirst, and all was quiet. The animals munched the grass, and Mujukuu kept watch over them. His grandpa fell off into a deep sleep, resting his head on a tree trunk. At least it was a quiet atmosphere for a nap.

The silence was, however, broken by the sudden noise of a cricket. 'It must be hiding in the crack on the bark of that tree!' shouted Mujukuu as he ran towards the tree.

He approached the tree stealthily and steadily peeped through the crack. The insect spread out its wing, rubbed its leg against the wing, and made another harsh creaky noise.

'That's creaky!' exclaimed Mujukuu's grandpa, who was wearing a frown on his face as he turned his head to look around.

At this time, Mujukuu wasn't sure whether his grandpa frowned because of the crick pain he used to experience in his neck or because of the disturbing creaky noise of the cricket. His grandpa was not amused with the way he had been disturbed from his nap, but instead of getting annoyed, he cracked a joke about the leaping chirping insect.

'We better get started; it's getting dark,' Mujuku's grandpa said as he arose from the ground.

Mukali, their guard dog, must have been hungry. He leaped after a bird that had just landed on the ground for its prey—the grasshopper. The bird escaped with its life. It was joined by a flock of other birds, and they all flew off into the sky. Poor Mukali! He was left gazing on.

Mujukuu joined Mukali in looking up the sky as he gently stroked the dog. The lavishing sunset on the horizon struck Mujukuu's eyes. Dusk was setting in, and it was getting creepy and scary out. Mukali made another mess, worsening the situation. Mukali leaped and stumbled over a stone, thrusting it into the river. He was going for a toad that had jumped ahead of him.

As the stone tumbled into the water, Mujukuu noticed something swim off. "A frog!" he screamed in fright. These creatures always scared him.

As they continued on the long journey home, Mujukuu noticed a colony of tiny ants creeping along the ground. These ants seemed to be on a mission as they marched on in one direction. They queued like well-organised soldiers and looked busy and yet overloaded with substances on their backs. They appeared to be seriously carrying their food, and Mujukuu had better leave them undisturbed!

The events of that evening seemed unusual to Mujukuu. When he went to bed, he could not help but reflect on the day. He had injured his leg earlier as he was running in the long grass, and the pain in his leg made this particular night longer than usual and intolerable. Just before dawn, when he thought of trying to catch some sleep, Mukali's antagonistic barking begun.

*The foxes must be on the farm again*! thought Mujukuu, tossing further in the bed. This seemed to be a night of rolling over and over in bed, while pondering life's issues. All that lingered in his mind were the lifestyles of the cricket, the grasshopper, the birds, the toad, the frog, the ants, and their dog Mukali. He clasped onto some insights from these!

Nearly a year had lapsed since Mujukuu's lifestyle had drastically changed. His dad was a primary school teacher, and his mum had lost her job and taken up a part-time job at a supermarket. It had become expensive for their parents to bring their family up in the city. If his parents had to put food on the table and, at the same time, save some funds for future use, then the best option was to send the children to the village. They had to live with their grandparents. Mujukuu had never liked this.

On this challenging night, Mujukuu emphasized accepting reality. He made up resolutions for the new leap year that was around the corner. He resolved to be content at his grandparents' home, just as the cricket and the grasshopper seemed gratified within their habitat. He would adapt to his new location, just as the toad and frog had adapted to their environments. He would cling to the family and move along with every member in the family, just like the flock of birds had flown up together. He would work hard and be focused like the ants. He would value the efforts of every member in the family, including Mukali's.

Nature had taught Mujukuu that he had a role to play in the family. After that night, his attitude changed remarkably and transcended the whole family's expectations. He comprehended that he himself was the determinant factor regarding life's horizons. His decision could only be compared to the parable of the two sons:

> *But what do you think? A man had two sons, and he came to the first and said, "Son, go, work today in my vineyard." He answered and said, "I will not," but afterward he regretted and went. Then he came to the second and said likewise. And he answered and said, "I go, sir," but he did not go. Which of the two did the will of the father?* (Mathew 21:28-31)

# 11

## Savings

'I will buy a birthday gift for my sister out of my own earnings,' declared Muteja one day.

As the day grew older, Muteja decided to speak to his dad about this nice toy that he had seen at the supermarket. Buying this toy with his own money would be a great achievement, but he did not have enough money yet. 'This would be the most suitable gift for my sister; she will be excited about it, and I must buy it,' he firmly declared.

His dad was left gazing at him in surprise.

The young boy smiled in return as his dad reassuringly dismissed him with a gentle pat on his back.

Muteja fancied this toy that he had seen at the supermarket. It was a teddy bear. The urge and the determination to purchase it could not be taken away from him. No one could persuade him from believing that it was the best possible gift for his sister. Though expensive, the toy was cuddly; it was cool-looking, and it was pink in colour. His sister was classy, her favourite colour was pink, and she preferred cuddly toys.

Muteja thought about the toy whenever he was at home, and every time he visited the supermarket, he could not stop admiring it. His biggest dream was to buy this ideal toy for his sister. He carried such an ambition and eagerness that everyone in the family was proud of him.

'Where will you get the money to buy such a costly teddy?' asked Muteja's concerned mum.

'I have a plan to achieve my goal,' Muteja boldly answered.

'Tell us the plan, young man,' his mum teased playfully whilst keeping her eyes fixed on the boy, as if to weed out any form of doubt.

'I will unpack and put away the shopping when we reach home, but for a little pay!' the boy replied. He said this precisely, his words and tone taking on the style of a radio broadcaster's announcement. He presented himself well, as if he were on a stage in front of an audience. He was as convincing as one who stands out in an interview with determination to get the job. He could only be compared to a young man who had set his mind on his career or his first paid job. If this was how he would earn the coins that would enable him get what he desired, then he knew that he had better do it right.

'That's brilliant and thoughtful,' his dad commended him.

'I am sure you understand how hard it is to put away the shopping, and especially after a tedious day like this,' his mum commented.

After every shopping outing, Muteja had always seen his dad drop copper coins in the coins cabinet. *These coins will soon drop in my hands*, he imagined, reaffirming his plan.

'Thank you for making the offer, and here is today's pay,' said Muteja's mum as she placed some copper coins in his hand.

His parents seemed to have better plans for the silver coins.

'Oh no; that means I won't have the copper coins for buying sweets and chocolates anymore!' objected Maua, Mutejah's sister.

'This won't be for long, my sister,' Muteja immediately answered. He had to distract his sister from thoughts that would thwart his skilful plan.

On Saturday morning, it was Maua's birthday. Muteja counted the copper coins in his piggy bank. His face suddenly went pale, and he looked bothered. One coin was missing; without it, he didn't have enough to purchase the teddy bear. He was careful not to disclose his secret to his sister. He mumbled words in frustration. This was the day he had looked forward to for so long, but something was amiss! Whatever the case, his dream had to come true; he was not going to give up or ask his parents to top up. He wanted to buy the toy out of his earnings.

He decided to engage in a search. Maua helplessly watched. He searched under the table, under the chairs, in the cushions, and in his pockets. Whatever it was that her brother searched for, Maua could see that it was not there.

Muteja shook the empty piggy bank, turned it over again and again, and looked through its hole, but nothing was there. He fetched a long broom that would reach the hidden areas underneath the furniture and thoroughly swept the floor. He then sat down as if to rest from the hard work, but he never relaxed. He searched in the rubbish as well until he found what he was looking for. He shouted in amazement and rejoiced like one bringing in the sheaves. He picked it up, wiped it, washed it, and put it together with the others; he had finally found the coin that had gone missing!

On his sister's birthday, Muteja was a proud and happy lad. He managed to buy his sister what had long been the purpose in his heart.

He never stopped putting pennies aside for rainy days. This earned him musical CDs, movie tickets, and extra money for fancy clothes.

Next, when it was his birthday, he received the gift he had always yearned for the silver coins that converted into notes. He deposited these into his personal savings account.

Maua emulated her brother and took over saving copper coins in the piggy bank.

Every coin was of importance in Muteja's count. There is a story in the Bible about a woman who valued her coin just like Muteja.

> '*Or what woman, having ten silver coins, if she loses one coin, does not light a lamp, sweep the house, and search carefully until she finds it? And when she has found it, she calls her friends and neighbors together, saying, "Rejoice with me, for I have found the piece which I lost"* (Luke 15:8-9).

# 12

## Time

The day was gone, but the effect of its tediousness lingered on. This day had seen many customers flow in and out of the workshop. A break from work was essential; Kijana's dad needed a moment away from the hustle of the day's activities. He yearned to recline on his chaise longue in the lounge. He would enjoy the fresh air in a home environment. Indeed, his son got it right when he noted that his father looked tired.

Inasmuch as Kijana's dad might have hoped to retire to bed, it was far too early for that. Kijana sat sunken into the couch besides him. Unlike the exhausted dad, the son's face looked fresh, and his actions remained energetic. His dad could tell that the lad's mind was still ready to absorb more information from the ongoing television programs.

'If only you would stop scrolling for more programs and go do your homework, Kijana!' his dad remarked.

The next day was Monday, and Kijana was supposed to hand in his homework, but he had not finished it. The essence of his dad's reminder never struck him!

That Monday evening, his dad came from work earlier than usual. Rather than follow his normal habit of sitting down to relax, he headed to the study room. He had a task to complete—a table to draw. He picked up a paper, a ruler, a rubber, and a pencil and started the drawing. Kijana joined him, his anticipation of seeing the drawing high. Only his eagerness faded away faster than expected. He recalled something and walked out of the room. He too had an assignment to complete.

'Dad,' called out Kijana on returning to the study room.

'Yes,' answered his dad, who was so engaged in his drawing that he never bothered to lift up his head and look at the boy.

'I have completed my homework, and I will hand it in tomorrow,' Kijana reported in excitement.

'It's good your class teacher did not mind the delay, but for your information, this does not go on the record as a good habit!" his dad sternly reprimanded him.

Perplexed by his dad's unexpected and serious reaction, the boy did not know what to say next. He, however, started to give reasons for the delay. He had thought of briefly watching the television, but without realizing how much time had passed, he found himself searching for more channels that interested him. He thought he had the whole weekend to finish his homework, but his cousin's visit had robbed him of the concentration and the time to settle down to task. From the look on his face, it was obvious that the boy was set to justify his actions further. His earlier excuses had been genuine, but as he continued, his excuses could only be classified as lame. Aiming to disrupt the boy's thoughtful mind, his dad summoned him to sit by him and join in, helping with the drawing. 'Fill in the table,' said his dad as he placed a simple chart, on the table before the boy.

Kijana drew the chart towards himself; it was his timetable!

On this, he allocated the times required for all his activities. The list of the activities seemed unending and yet turned out to be an organized list that included playtime, television programs, meetings with his friends and grandparents, end of term dates, birthdays, and games times.

In appreciation for the time Kijana had put in to fill in the timetable, his dad gave him three brand new items—an alarm clock, a wristwatch, and a diary. These are the tools that aided Kijana in gaining the skills of efficient time management.

Thrilled by the final fine art, he resolved to display the timetable on the wall in his bedroom. This was the best idea, since he needed to refer to it daily and plan the day ahead. When he became accustomed to using this time management tool, he always handed in his homework on time. The timetable had worked. He understood the importance of time management for the rest of his life.

The Bible talks about the importance of managing one's time well and completing one's tasks. For example, we read in Luke:

*And the lord said, 'Who then is that faithful and wise steward, whom his master will make ruler over his household, to give them their portion of food in due season? Blessed is that servant whom his master will find so doing when he comes. Truly, I say to you that he will make him ruler over all that he has. But if that servant says in his heart, "My master is delaying his coming," and begins to beat the male and the female servants, and to eat and drink and be drunk, the master of that servant will come on a day when he is not looking for him, and at an hour when he is not aware, and will cut him in two and appoint him his portion with the unbelievers. And that servant who knew his master's will, and did not prepare himself or do according to his will, shall be beaten with many stripes.* (Luke 12:42-47).

# 13

## Family

Summer was at its peak, and the heat of the day was intolerable. Staying indoors was uncomfortable. A gentle and a cool breeze on my soft skin were two things that I yearned for. Dad had resolved himself to lying on a mat under the shade of the tree in our backyard and taking a nap. As I looked through the window, I could only admire him. Joining him would mean disturbing his peaceful rest. The house was quiet. Mum and my little sister had gone shopping.

I never fancied accompanying them. It wasn't that I didn't like shopping. Rather, my little sister, 'the princess of the family', throwing tantrums and crying for almost every toy at the supermarket always put me off and embarrassed me.

At last, I decided to inch towards Dad, being cautious not to awaken him. I blankly and silently sat down beside him. I almost dozed off, until I decided to engage in some drawing and colouring. The *ding-dong* of the door bell followed by a knock at the door aroused Dad from sleep. I ran to open the door.

On returning, I found him drawing. A closer look at the drawing, and I saw that he had drawn a sketch of a tree. On second look, I saw that the drawing had the exact configurations of the tree we sat under. Dad was a perfect artist. Drawing and colouring were not only part of the skills he had acquired but natural talents too. Most of the pictures that hanged in our house were his artistic work. He intended to make another picture for our sitting room. I keenly observed his drawing and concentrated on every detail of the decorations and the colourings.

'It's beautiful; it's a Christmas tree!' I exclaimed in delight.

'Not this time,' he replied.

The pretty and colourful tree was of a value that surpassed the Christmas trees that we threw away after the season!

On finalizing the drawing, he made a list of important components of both trees and humans. The terms included trunk, roots, origins, backgrounds, branching, crossbreeding, migration, spread, bearing, fruits, seeds, pruning, reproduction, living, regenerate, species, and genes. I yawned as I thought of how Dad had decided get me into a biology class.

He then reached for a folded piece of paper from his pocket. He spread it on the ground after gently unfolding it. It was a list of our family's names, some of which I did not recognize at all. He carefully drew boxes and filled them in with certain names; finally, he drew lines connecting each box to the other boxes. He gave a precise explanation of why he had made the list of terms that applied to both trees and humans beings. If you have ever heard of 'The Tree of Jesse' in the museums and on church buildings, then you understand that my Dad had drawn 'Our Family Tree!'

The Tree of Jesse is an artistic depiction of the ancestors of Christ, shown in a tree that rises from Jesse of Bethlehem, the father of King David; this was the first time a 'family tree' was used to represent genealogy.

I stored a copy of this valid information on the computer, framed another, and embossed the third copy on the wall. These important documents were for future reference; I can update the chart, making it possible to trace, locate, and reunite biological families. I felt pleasure when I stayed under the canopy of the physical tree that provided shelter from the heat of the day. But the joy I found in knowing that I was part of our abiding family tree was more satisfying. There is more pleasure in aligning oneself with the Lord Jesus Christ, for He is the true vine:

> *I am the true vine, and My Father is the vine dresser. Every branch in Me that does not bear fruit He takes away; and every branch that bears fruit He prunes, that it may bear more fruit. You are already clean because of the word which I have spoken to you. Abide in Me, and I in you. As the branch cannot bear fruit of itself, unless it abides in the vine, neither can you, unless you abide in Me. I am the vine, you are the branches. He who abides in Me, and I in him, bears much fruit; for without Me you can do nothing. If anyone does not abide in Me, he is cast out as a branch and is withered; and they gather them and throw them into the fire, and they are burned. If you abide in Me, and My words abide in you, you will ask what you desire, and it shall be done for you. By this My Father is glorified, that you bear much fruit; so you will be My disciples. As the Father loved Me, I also have loved you; abide in My love.* (John 15:1-9).

# CONCLUSION

The lot of every child needs to follow after this verse: '*All your children shall be taught by the LORD, and great shall be the peace of your children*' (Isaiah 54:13).